How To Buy A Property

How To Buy A Property

A Simple Guide for Millennials

Lildonia McNally Lawrence
and
Cory McNally

How to Buy a Property: A Simple Guide for Millennials

Artwork: © Amahl McLaughlin

ISBN: 1976072735
ISBN 13: 9781976072734

Contents

About the Authors

Lildonia Lawrence author of *How to Buy a Property: A Simple Guide for Millennials* is a life coach and well-being professional. Her background is within in the support industry, mainly within education and the health sector. Lildonia's work involves supporting people to achieve their goals professionally, personally and physically, whether that be through teaching group classes, workshops, courses or working with clients one-to-one.

To find out more about Lildonia's work, see: www.movewithlildonia.com

Cory McNally researcher of *How to Buy a Property: A Simple Guide for Millennials* is a lettings manager working at a leading estate agency in the central London lettings market. His property journey began aged 21, when he started working as a sales agent in a local agency. He loved it and quickly began plotting and planning how he himself could enter the property market.

Cory is a registered agent with ARLA Propertymark (formally, the Association of Residential Lettings Agents), and has a wealth of knowledge about the property market and lettings scene.

Introduction

Welcome to *How to Buy a Property: A Simple Guide for Millennials*! We're thrilled that you've chosen to read this book, and hope you will get lots of information to help you along your property journey. This book is your one-stop shop for all things property purchase.

It's a simple and easy-to-read guide that will lead you through information about the property market and how you can make it work for you. We'll cover all the big topics, such as securing a mortgage, saving a deposit, government schemes and how to find (and buy) your ideal home. We've aimed this book at the everyday millennial and young professional – just like us!

Millennial (*noun*)
Also known as 'Generation Y' or the 'Net Generation'.
The term usually applies to individuals who reached
adulthood within the turn of the 21st century.
Broadly speaking, those born 1980–2000

So, who are we, and why did we write this book?

First, we are not multimillion pound property magnates, high-flying CEOs, bankers or the children of wealthy landowners. We are just two 1980s-born folks who needed a place to live after university, and wanted some security in our adult lives.

Our journey began when we graduated from Brunel University in 2010, with nowhere to live. For various reasons our childhood homes were unavailable for us to move back into, and we needed somewhere to stay – fast. Our requirements were fairly simple: we needed somewhere with easy access to central London, and with close proximity to our current jobs.

We ended up finding a flat the size of a matchbox for £750 a month, above a parade of shops in a suburban high street. It was so small that we could vacuum it in its entirety without unplugging the cleaner once. Our bedroom was so tiny that you couldn't open the wardrobe and the bedroom door at the same time. Our bathroom was so minute that... you get the picture. It was small!

In spite of this, we were happy. We'd found somewhere in a decent location that we could call our own. We got on fairly well for the first week or so, until the noise started. The restaurant below was constantly holding shindigs, and the sound would reverberate up to our little flat and into the wee hours of the morning. During the day wasn't much better, as the street below was often extremely loud – and the constant passing of buses meant we inhaled noxious exhaust fumes if we dared to open the window.

The final straw came when we opened our front door to find that a family of oversized and obnoxious looking rats had set up camp outside. It gave us both the heebie-jeebies, and after further inspection and moving various bins, we found hundreds more squirming around in the poorly distributed rubbish of our 'favourite' restaurant...

We spent the next few months sleep-deprived and panicked, trying our best to catnap during the day and dodge mutant rodents during the evening. We can laugh about it now, but at the time it was a horrendous experience. Coupled with the fact that we were only a few months into our graduate jobs, it was a very stressful time.

We didn't last very long in that flat, and begged our landlord to break our tenancy: luckily she obliged, and we were able to leave. It was at that point we decided that we would never rent again, and that the only way forward was to purchase our own property.

We're happy to say that we have managed to achieve our goal more than once, and the impact it has had on our well-being has been amazing. The security that having your own roof over your head brings is epic. It's such a relief not to have to worry about dodgy landlords shirking their responsibilities, or drunken roommates eating all of your cheese!

Unfortunately, our story isn't unique. We have so many friends and colleagues who are either forced to live at home or in uncomfortable situations because they feel unable to purchase their own home. In our opinion, this is not on. If someone wants to purchase a home and is willing to put in the work, they should be able to do that.

Often, millennials are dubbed as 'eternal teenagers' – and in some ways that is true. But with barriers such as increasing unemployment rates, rising university tuition fees and mounting property prices, it's genuinely hard for young adults to learn to stand on their own two feet.

We've learned a whole heap along the way, and are always getting questions from our peers, asking how they too can make the big leap in home owner-ship – which is why we decided to write this book. We love helping people, and want to share our learning with as many as possible, particularly those who feel that owning their own home is an unobtainable goal.

However, our journey wasn't straightforward. We were 22 at the time of our first purchase; all of our respective families were in social housing, and all of our friends were living at home. We had no one to ask for advice, and all the material we came across both online and in print was aimed at large-scale property investors, with thousands of pounds at their disposal. We didn't even know where to start. Had we had access to a book like this, we're certain we would have read it from cover-to-cover.

Things are getting harder: the average age of a first-time buyer has risen to 31, and the vast majority are only able to buy with help from their families. Many young people are getting frozen out of the market, with first-time buyers putting down an average deposit of £53,000. This is more than twice the average full-time salary for 22 to 29-year-olds, which is £21,609.[1] It is not surprising that many millennials feel that owning their home is out of reach, but we want to let you know that this is not the case. It may not be easy, but where there is a will, there is a way – and if you *have* the will, we'll indeed show you the way!

You can use this guide in any way you choose, from picking out the bits that excite you the most, to choosing what you feel is most relevant. However, we suggest simply starting at the beginning and reading all the way through. Everything that is here has been included for a reason, and we wouldn't want you to miss out on any valuable information.

---

1   Tijvan Pettinger (2016) 'UK Housing Market', Economics Help, 8 April. Retrieved 21 August 2017, www.economicshelp.org/blog/5709/housing/market/; see also Office for National Statistics.

Throughout the book we'll be throwing lots of industry-specific terms your way. They are marked in bold in the text, and you can check out their definitions in our handy glossary at the back of the book. We've also included tips and examples right the way through, so you'll be able to see our advice in a real life context.

So please sit back, relax and enjoy. We look forward to seeing where this journey takes you!

Chapter 1

● ● ●

Why to Buy?

Trends in the property market

Property is the topic of the moment and investment is high on many people's radar, as well as big on the Government's agenda. So, what is all the fuss about buying? Why can't we simply be like our European cousins, and rent for life?

Well, the main reason is because in the UK, property and land is the dominant and most consistent way of building and sustaining wealth. Let's take a look at the facts.

Figure 1: Average UK house prices, 1970–2016

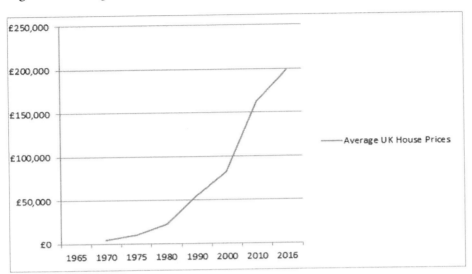

As you can see, the percentage increase of the value of property is enormous. Traditionally, property has been known to double in value roughly every eight to 10 years. This has been the case throughout the last century, and is set to continue.

There will always be people who say the property market will eventually crash, fall or decline. However, there is no reason to suggest that this will happen, based on historical upward movement of the property market. Even if this were the case, there is no reason to suggest that that this trend will *suddenly* change. Of course there are regional variations and fluctuations in price, but these statistics give a macro view of property trends in the entirety of the UK.

As property tends to rise steadily in value, your home can make you money and serve as an asset.

> **Example**
>
> A lucky homeowner bought a property in the 1970s worth £4,321. They were £194,000 better off in 2016 – which would take a lifetime to save. If they had saved £200 a month for 47 years, they would only have reached a total of £112,800.
>
> Considering that salaries in 1970 were a lot lower than they are now, that would have been pretty difficult to achieve. For an everyday individual in the 1970s with an everyday job, property was a sure-fire way to build wealth.

This scenario still rings true today. An individual on a £28,000 salary who purchases a property will be generally much wealthier in 20 years than someone on a consistent salary of £100,000 with no assets. This is because the asset is increasing in value day-by-day, whereas the person on the fixed salary is tied to their job and wage. If a high earner loses their job, they will have nothing bar perhaps some savings, whereas the person with property will have an asset that earns for them consistently.

Equity

This leads us nicely to our next point, which is the concept of **equity.** Equity is the difference between the value of a property and what is left outstanding in the form of a mortgage. Equity is your golden ticket to property heaven: it is what developers and individual purchasers chase alike, as it is the core element that creates wealth.

In fact, 'equity' and 'wealth' are generally interchangeable concepts. They are completely separate to how much a person earns, how much they have in savings or how they spend their money.

Essentially, equity is a bank account built into your property, where its worth is stored. Let's look at some examples.

Example 1: Property value of £100,000

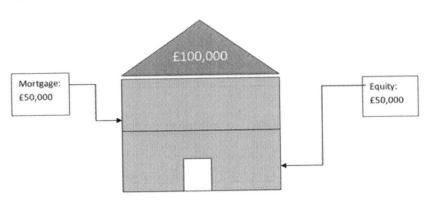

If you own a property worth £100,000 with a mortgage of £50,000, your equity amounts to £50,000. So, if you were to sell your property (all associated fees aside), in theory the money you would have left over is £50,000 in hard cash. Without selling, the £50,000 is still present but it is tied up within the property – therefore you don't have access to it. (There are other ways to release this equity without selling, which we will talk about later in Chapter 7.)

Example 2: Property value of £200,000

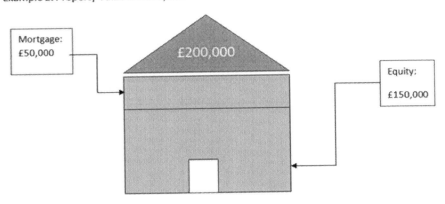

Using this example, if the same property were to double in value to £200,000, your equity would increase threefold to £150,000 (£200,000 – £50,000 mortgage = £150,000). This is irrespective of how much you earn, how much you've saved or any other factors relating to your earning potential. Owning property can effectively take you out of **The Matrix**, and release you from the notion that you make money by having a good job and a high wage – which is what many of us still believe.

As you can see, building equity within property is a guaranteed way to increase your wealth, both in assets and potentially in real-life cash terms. The more equity within your property, the wealthier you are.

Leverage

Now we've got to grips with equity, it's time to move on to the notion of **leverage.** Leverage is using other people's money (namely, the bank) to provide a greater return on your investment. In a nutshell: the more money you borrow, the higher leverage you have.

This is also present in the business world, as this example shows.

> **Example**
>
> You take out a start-up business loan of £10,000 to open a shop. You buy stock, hire staff and start to sell your products. You make £30,000 after the first year.
>
> You pay back the bank (with interest) at £14,000, and have made a profit of the remaining £16,000:

$$£30,000 – £14,000 = £16,000$$

Without the initial start-up loan you wouldn't have been able to make that profit. Therefore, you have used the loan as leverage to provide a return. With property it is exactly the same.

Let's take a look at a theoretical example.

> **Example**
>
> You put down a 10% deposit of £10,000 on a property worth £100,000. The bank lends you the remaining 90% = £90,000.
>
> The property goes up in value over two years to £120,000, but you still only owe £90,000.
>
> $$£120,000 - £90,000 = £30,000$$
>
> $$£30,000 - £10,000 \text{ original deposit} = £20,000 \text{ increase in value}$$

In the above example, this would mean that you've accumulated a 20% increase for yourself in the form of an extra £20,000. That's a 200% return on investment, with only a 20% increase in value!

If you were to put the same £10,000 into stocks, shares or material items and the value increased by 20% to 12,000, you would be left with an increase of only £2,000. Compare this with the £10,000 used to invest in property and, as you can see, there is potential to make an awful lot more.

Of course, in real life things are a lot more complex than our basic examples here, but these figures do illustrate the possibilities that investing in the property market can offer.

It's important to mention that there are many other factors to consider, such as additional costs and property value. The figures for return on investment will vary greatly depending on mortgage rate, location and property. It's also important to note that there are ongoing maintenance costs associated with owning property. However, looking back at the general trends, the average property now is worth a lot more then it was 10 years ago, regardless of initial purchase price or location.

As we mentioned earlier, some people worry about prospective market crashes and reductions in property value during economic downturn. The property market is cyclical, and there is always a chance that an investment will go down. However, if it is a long-term investment you are looking for, this shouldn't be too much of a cause for concern. Considering the history of the property market and its present-day trajectory, property prices are set to rise. This has been previously consistent, despite the occasional blip. Hold on to your property long enough, and it should go up in value.

So, considering the factors of why *people* buy, it's time to figure out why *you* want to buy. Have a go at our 'Why to Buy' quiz to figure out your buying motivation.

Quiz: Why do you want to buy?

1. Why are you reading this book?
   a) I want to become a multimillion pound property investor!
   b) I need somewhere to live
   c) I'm vaguely interested in the possibility of property as an earner
2. What is your main motivation for wanting to buy?
   a) Financial all the way – I want a good income
   b) I'm looking to settle down in one place
   c) I don't want to live at home forever
3. How soon do you need to move?
   a) It's not urgent, but I can't stay where I am forever
   b) Like, yesterday!
   c) I'm quite happy where I am for now

4. How does buying a property fit into your long-term plans?
    a) I want to work for myself, and I see the property market as a potential way to make that happen
    b) I want somewhere I can live for the foreseeable future
    c) I'm not too sure yet
5. What are your thoughts on **'flipping'** a property?
    (Flipping is purchasing a property and selling it on quickly, with the sole aim of making a profit.)
    a) I'd love to give it a go – I watch those property shows and it looks great!
    b) It sounds awful, way too much stress!
    c) It looks like a lot of work, but it's something I would consider
6. Would you consider becoming a landlord?
    a) I would – it looks like a great way to earn an income
    b) Not at the moment, I've got too much on with work/family and other commitments
    c) I'm not averse to it – I'd like to find out more

Mostly As: Future property guru

Let's just call you Mr/Ms Hotshot Homeowner! It's clear you've got a passion for property and that you want to make a living from being an investor. There is no reason why you can't have that. Feel free to use this book as a springboard to find out the ins-and-outs of property purchase, before moving on to property investment-specific books.

Mostly Bs: Homely homebod

You want somewhere comfortable to lay your head at night. That's a fantastic plan, and something to which many people can relate. Use this book as a guide to make an airtight plan to find your perfect home.

Mostly Cs: Adaptable abode owner

You're open to the opportunities that owning property can bring. You may not be in a rush to leave where you are, so you can use this book to take your time and decide the right plan for your property journey.

As you can see from our very scientific quiz, there are three main routes to take when purchasing property:

1. As an investment
2. As a home
3. As a mixture of both.

We're going to go through all three in detail to help you figure out exactly which feels right for you. Once you've worked out your motivation for buying, it is important to keep your goal in mind when making any grand plans – especially those which involve spending great big wads of cash.

Property as an investment

This is probably the most talked-about type of purchase, and it is based on the previously described idea of leverage. Property as an investment can be extremely lucrative, and there are fantastic gains to be made. There are many different routes and strategies into making a living from investment: we have highlighted three of the most popular types:

1. The Big Flipper
2. The Landlord
3. The Off-Plan Chancer.

1. The Big Flipper

Big Flippers buy property and increase its value through renovation and refurbishment. Then they sell it on for more than the total cost of the purchase price (including works done).

Pros:

* Short-term – flipping can be a relatively quick process
* Potential for large gains.

Cons:

* Risky – there is no guarantee that your work will increase the property to the value you desire
* Complex – there are multiple factors to consider such as budget, architectural design, managing trades people, planning permission, sales potential and fees.

2. The Landlord

Landlords buy a property, keep hold of it and rent it out. The rental income should cover all costs associated with the property, plus a little on top. The longer you retain the property, the higher the value. This means that once you have built enough equity, you can **remortgage** and purchase another property, while retaining the first. This process can be repeated many times until a stable income is reached.

Pros:

* A safer strategy – less risk is involved, with a more straightforward route to building equity

* Simple model – it can be upscaled as time progresses
* Potential for a large and stable income.

Cons:

* Long-term – unless you have many properties, one to two rental units usually will not provide you with enough income to live off. Acquiring numerous properties can take many years
* You have to deal with finding tenants, estate agent fees and other ongoing costs and responsibilities associated with property management.

3. The Off-Plan Chancer

Some investors choose to buy **off-plan** from large property development companies. Developers invest a high amount into designing a complex, and need to raise a certain amount of capital before they can build. In order to do this, they sell off as many units as possible before the build at a relatively low price. Investors buy one or more incomplete units in a block of **new builds**, and sell them once the development has been built.

(NB: This is not something we've personally tried or have much experience of, but it is out there as an option.)

Pros:

* Possibility for an easy return once the property is built, as you can simply sell it and move on
* Instant equity.

Cons:

* Uncertainty – you are spending thousands of pounds on something that won't be completed for two to three years, possibly longer
* If the developer runs out of money, sometimes building work is delayed.

Property as a home

This is the other side of the coin, and was where we were when we first started. Initially we just wanted a safe, comfortable and welcoming place to live. For some, buying a property is simply about having a secure base where they can reside for the foreseeable future. This is the majority of people in the first-time buyers' market.

Pros:

* Escape the feeling that you're throwing away money on rent
* Complete autonomy over your living space – e.g. decoration, fixtures and fittings
* Long-term security, as long as you can afford your mortgage.

Cons:

* You are responsible for anything that falls into disrepair with the property
* Earning potential with one property as a home is limited.

Property as a mixture of both

In this case, people may have their primary residence and one or two rental homes that supplement their income, or provide a cosy nest egg for the future.

Pros:

* All of the same pros as property as a home –a lovely, stable home with which you can build equity
* A greater level of security than owning the one property
* Supplementary income from rental proceeds.

Cons:

* Need to be a good multi-tasker – focusing on managing your rental properties, home and potentially still holding down full-time work.

Here, we will be focusing on the latter two options. We want to support the everyday person: from the individual who just wants a really lovely home, to the person who is also interested in a 'side hustle' in the form of a rental income, and everyone in-between.

Case studies

Let's have a look at some real stories and how they fared when trying to become homely home bods and adaptable abode owners.

• • •

Sasha, 59

Sasha had known she wanted to buy a property for as long as she could remember. When she had her first child at 32, she was granted a three-bedroom council house. Although the house was perfect for them, she didn't have **right to buy**, and applied for a **council swap**. Her request was granted, and Sasha ended up in a lovely top-floor converted flat in a desirable area.

Having been a council tenant for a long period of time, Sasha qualified for a substantial discount on her deposit, so she saved up and bought the flat. She lived there happily for a number of years until her children reached their late teens. It was at this point that Sasha decided that she wanted to live abroad. She had built up a large amount of equity in her flat, so she decided to rent it out and buy another smaller abode in an exotic location.

Before renting out the flat, Sasha chose to complete some home improvements, and remortgaged the property. However, as she received a large amount of cash from the remortgaging, she began to overspend. She designed the flat very personally, as if she were going to live in it herself, rather than preparing the property for tenants.

Unfortunately, by the end of the refurbishment she had no contingency funds left. Sasha was forced to sell her property. As the property market had increased she had no money left to buy a replacement flat, and now has to rent a place to live.

• • •

Sonny and Samantha, 32

When Sonny and Samantha got engaged, Samantha lived with flatmates and Sonny lived at home with parents. They knew they wanted a family home for the future – somewhere they could stay for many years, and in which to raise a family.

After getting married, they decided to move in with Sonny's parents to save for a deposit. Sonny's parents allowed them to stay at home rent-free, meaning that the couple could save up to £2,000 a month. They both had reasonably paid jobs, and were able to save this amount comfortably. They treated themselves to one large holiday a year, but they did not go out much, ate most meals at home, and made social occasions as inexpensive as possible.

After six years Sonny and Samantha had saved enough for a deposit on their property. They now live in a three-bedroom house, in a town close to Sonny's parents. They are looking forward to starting a family in a stable base.

• • •

Aoife, 29

Aoife was keen to move out of her parents' flat: she wanted her own space and some security for the future. She made a plan to save up a deposit for a flat in two years, with a plan to buy before her 30th birthday.

Aoife had a successful career in London, but she decided to move to the Middle East so that she could earn a tax-free salary in a short time frame. She worked as a nanny, meaning that her accommodation, food and often travel was included.

When Aoife returned from the Middle East after a year, she had saved £30,000 – which was more than enough of a deposit for a flat in her home town on the outskirts of London. Aoife moved back in with her parents in order to start her property search. However, she missed the buzz of the city, and when a friend had a spare room going in a flatshare in London, Aoife couldn't resist. She moved back to the city and began paying £900 a month in rent. That, plus nights out and a return to a lower taxable income, meant that after one year Aoife had spent her savings, and was now back to square one.

Sadly, Aoife had to move back in with her parents. She has taken up bar work alongside her full-time job in order to start saving again.

• • •

Lacey, 34

Lacey was 25 when she decided to buy a property. She didn't mind where she lived, but she knew that she didn't want to live with her parents forever. Lacey was working part-time and studying. She began saving small amounts of money each month. She also contributed a small amount to her parents for rent, so began working on the weekends in order to supplement her wage.

By the time that she was 29, Lacey had saved up enough money to begin her property search. Price point was her main guide, and she was able to find a flat about 10 miles from where she grew up. She was happy as the price was within her range, but she could still easily access her friends and family by car. Lacey knew that she couldn't quite afford to move out just yet, so she decided to rent out the property while continuing to live at home.

After five years, and once Lacey was working full-time, she decided to move into the property and make it her home. As Lacey had built up a large amount of equity in her property, she was able to release some cash to do up the flat before she moved in. Lacey stayed focused on the goal of moving out of her parents' house, and was able to achieve it.

• • •

As you can see, the people who kept to a game plan were the most successful on their property journey. Once you have figured out what path you want your property journey to take, the next step is focusing on creating a goal. This is your *final destination*: the destination you will think of with every single action you take.

For example, if you are planning to rent out your property, don't kit it out with uber-trendy, expensive furniture. Conversely, if you want a long-term home, stick to viewing properties in areas in which you could see yourself living, as opposed to areas of high investment potential.

Creating your SMART goal

This is the point where you solidify your goals and aims. Your first step is to create a SMART goal. These are criteria used to set goals in the fields of professional and personal development.

SMART goals are useful, as they cover all aspects of your plans and provide a framework for you to work with. SMART stands for:

Specific

Measurable

Achievable

Realistic

Time-framed.

Here is an example of a SMART, property-focused goal:

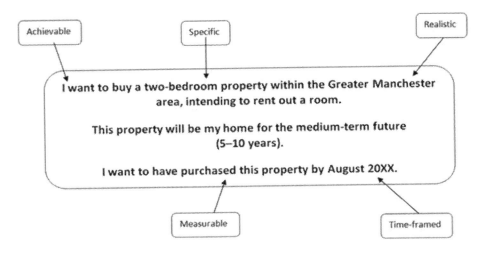

Specific – There is no point being vague about things: be precise, and nail down exactly what you want. For example, change 'I want to buy a property' to 'I want to buy a two-bedroom property within the Greater Manchester area, intending to rent out a room'.

Measurable – Make sure you've always got a marker to go by: how will you know you've achieved your goal overall? For most of you it will be when you've bought your property, but depending on your goal it could be, for example, 'When I've got a tenanted property'.

Achievable – Is your goal achievable? For example, are you able to buy a property if you are currently a newly-qualified professional trying to get your first step on the career ladder? Probably not. In this instance, perhaps an initial goal would be saving towards a deposit.

Realistic – How realistic is your goal? If you're crippled with debt, perhaps this is not practical right now, so the goal might need to be clearing any monies owed first.

Time-framed – All great goals need to be time-framed. This is a fantastic point of reference against which to check your progress.

Creating your action plan

Once you've got your SMART goal in place, the next step is to create an action plan. Using the example above, this person may have a long way to go to get to their end goal. Their action plan may start with the simple step of having a chat with a mortgage adviser to find out what they can realistically afford on their salary.

With a suitable action plan drawn up, then you can start devising mini-goals to get you there. For example, a simple initial action for the above would be:

Speak with an independent mortgage adviser about my options and budget by [XX] date.

It's important to break your final goal into small, attainable steps. This way it will not become too overwhelming, and you can give yourself a little pat on the back every time you reach a milestone.

We've included more information on what to do once you've established your goal in the next chapter, but for now, think about where you want to end up, and what you want your SMART goal to be.

My Smart Goal:

Conclusion

Remember to review your SMART goal regularly. Things change, and goals may need to be tweaked, re-examined and, on occasion, completely overhauled. That's fine: the most important thing is to have a goal and an action plan from which to work. Whatever you do, stick to the plan, and don't lose sight of the final destination!

Notes

Chapter 2

● ● ●

First Things First: Where to Start?

So, now you've got your SMART goal sorted, it's time to get down to the nitty gritty. This chapter considers the first steps you need to take, as well as the individual things for which you will need to save. We will cover everything you need to know to secure a mortgage and the different types of mortgages. We'll also cover tips on saving for a deposit, budgeting and the support you'll need to get your finances in order.

The mortgage

The majority of property questions we receive are about mortgages. Many people question what they can afford, and how difficult it is to get one. We all have varying circumstances, which include different salary levels, working structures (employee, self-employed, contractor) and deposit amounts.

Talk to a mortgage adviser

The only sure-fire way to answer your mortgage questions is to speak with a mortgage adviser. A mortgage adviser is a trained professional who will assess your financial situation and find you the best mortgage deal. There are mortgage advisers within banks who will only show you the mortgages that their bank offer, and there are independent mortgage advisers who will scour hundreds of different lenders in order to find you the best deal.

Independent mortgage advisers are just like human comparison sites: they work for you, the client, not lenders. Often people resist seeing a mortgage adviser out of fear that he/she will judge them if they don't have thousands of pounds behind them. On the contrary: this is the best thing to do, as you can only develop your saving targets once you know how much of a mortgage you could be granted.

TIP: The easiest way to find a mortgage adviser is to call around local estate agents – they will always have good contacts with brokers in your area.

Mortgage advisers will not usually charge you a fee. They are paid mainly by the lender, who supplies you with a mortgage – so their input to you as a customer is free at the point of use. Later down the line, when you've secured a mortgage and purchased a property, there is usually a small fee of around £1,000 to £1,500 from the bank. However, this can be added to your monthly mortgage repayments, and does not need to be paid up front.

Proof of earnings

When you meet with a mortgage adviser, they will ask you how much you have in savings, and for evidence of your annual salary if you're employed (usually three payslips). If you're buying with friends, family or a partner, they will take into account the total income from all parties concerned.

> **Example**
>
> Most lenders are willing to lend roughly five times the annual salary of the potential purchasers.
>
> Say you have a salary of £25,000 and your partner, friend or co-purchaser has a similar salary, the bank should be willing to give you a mortgage of around £250,000:
>
> £25,000 + £25,000 = £50,000
>
> £50,000 x 5 = £250,000

If you are a contractor or self-employed, usually you will have to provide three years' tax returns in order to prove that you have a stable and regular income.

Be honest with your adviser

When working with a mortgage adviser, the most important thing is to be open and honest. There is no point inflating savings or salaries in the hope that they won't notice. This is their job, and you will have to provide evidence for all your financials anyway! It is important that you have a good rapport with them, and that they have a thorough understanding of your personal situation and what exactly you are looking for.

Along with local estate agents, your mortgage adviser should become a favourite in your contact list. You should be able to discuss ideas with them openly and honestly. If you feel that the chemistry isn't there, find someone else. You are not bound to one adviser, and the most important thing is that you feel understood. The more you click with your adviser, the more likely they are to work for you and to support you to secure the best mortgage deal.

Choosing a mortgage

Once your mortgage adviser has assessed and analysed your situation, they will get to work finding some mortgage offers for you. Mortgages are offered over a period of time, usually 25 to 35 years. This is called the **mortgage term**, and signifies how long you will have to pay it back.

As well as the overall term, nearly every mortgage offer will come with a specific time frame attached to the terms of that particular deal. This can range from one to five years, and is similar to a mobile phone contract. You're locked in under the same terms for that time frame, but when the term ends you are free to find a new (and hopefully better) deal.

Once your mortgage adviser has found some options that suit, and you have decided to move forward with that particular product, your mortgage offer lasts for just three months. If you haven't found a property within three months, it's important to go back to your mortgage adviser to renew it: this way, you won't get caught short when you do find a property that you like.

Interest

All mortgage products will come with an additional cost, and that is the **interest rate**. This is the cost you will pay each year (in monthly instalments) to borrow the money. This works exactly the same as a car loan or a store card, etc.

> **Example**
>
> Say you have a £100,000 mortgage with a 3% interest rate.
>
> £100,000 x 3% = £3,000 a year in interest, spread out over the year.
>
> This will be included in your monthly mortgage payment, and is something you will be made aware of by your mortgage adviser.

Banks work out your interest rate based on what they refer as a **Loan to Value (LTV)**, which is how the banks calculate the risk on lending.

> **Example**
>
> A 10% deposit of a £100,000 property = a mortgage of £90,000, with a LTV of 90%. This means you will have a 90% mortgage.
>
> A 20% deposit gives you an 80% LTV mortgage. A 30% deposit gives you a 70% LTV.

The lower the LTV figure is, the more competitive the interest rate on the mortgage, and the cheaper your repayments will be.

Types of mortgage

When looking at your mortgage choices, there are four main types you can access:

1. Fixed-rate mortgage
2. Tracker mortgage
3. Standard variable rate mortgage
4. Remortgage.

1. Fixed-rate mortgage

This mortgage does exactly what it says on the tin. The rate you pay in interest every month is fixed for a period of time. Lots of people like this option, as they feel secure in the knowledge that their mortgage payments will be the same every single month.

An example of this would be a mortgage offer of 3% fixed for two years. Generally, the longer the fixed term, the higher the interest rate. The positive aspect of a fixed-rate mortgage is that you pay a set amount each month, regardless of economic changes in the market. However, if the **Bank of England base rate** is low then you could be paying over the odds, as your fixed rate will be higher than the 'standard'. Having said this, should the base rate increase, you will not be affected while on a fixed-rate mortgage.

2. Tracker mortgage

These mortgages are related to the Bank of England base rate. The fee you pay is a set margin above or below the base rate.

Example

If the base rate is 0.5% and a tracker deal is offering a mortgage of 2% interest, you will end up paying a rate of 2.5%:

$$0.5\% + 2\% = 2.5\%$$

When the base rate changes, the rate you pay will go up (or down) accordingly. So, for example, if the base rate rises to 1%, you would pay 3%.

If it falls to 0.25%, you would pay 2.25%.

Tracker deals are available for two, three or five years. Also, you could opt for a lifetime tracker deal instead, which tracks the base rate throughout the entire term of the mortgage. When interest rates are low, you could end up paying quite a lot less than a fixed term mortgage. On the flipside, if interest rates go up, you could end paying quite a lot more.

3. Standard variable rate mortgage

This is essentially the mortgage equivalent of a 'no-strings attached' relationship. You are able to change deals as you please without any penalty.

This is the type of mortgage that most banks will put you on after you've completed the set time frame of a fixed rate or tracker mortgage deal. It means that you can change to a new deal whenever you feel like, leading to greater flexibility than other options. However, these mortgages usually have a higher rate of interest than deals which are locked into a particular time frame.

4. Remortgage

This just means that your existing mortgage deal has come to an end and that you are free to choose a new deal. Often, when remortgaging, you get a better interest rate as you should have built up equity within your property. This is because now you will be taking a smaller loan from the bank: you've paid off a certain amount over the previous mortgage term, and the LTV is lower than it was at the start, meaning better rates.

Repaying your mortgage

Once you've chosen your mortgage offer, you will have options to pay it back. This is called the **mortgage repayment**, and there are two main types:

1. standard repayment mortgage
2. interest-only mortgage.

Standard repayment mortgage

This repayment schedule is what you choose when you want all of your payments to contribute to paying off your mortgage. As we've discussed, all mortgages come with an interest rate, which means that you will be paying off more then you've borrowed. This is how the bank makes its money.

With a standard repayment mortgage, the monthly payment will be split (usually unevenly) between **capital payments** and interest:

* Capital payments – the money actually paying down the final figure you owe the bank
* Interest –the cost you pay to the bank for lending the money.

Monthly payments are often split, with a larger proportion being paid towards interest during the first few years of a mortgage, so only a small proportion will go to paying down your mortgage in the initial years.

Some years later, this balance will shift so that a larger proportion of your monthly payment is towards capital repayment. The reason for this partition is down to the banks. Many people **remortgage** after a few years, and so the banks want to optimise their return in the form of the investment. Some people find it disheartening that their mortgage won't go down much in the first few years, but as with everything, it's important to think of the long game. If you keep paying off a mortgage month-by-month on a standard repayment, eventually it will come to an end and you will be mortgage-free!

Interest-only mortgage

This option means that over the entire term of the mortgage you do not pay any off anything that you've borrowed. With this type of repayment you only pay off the interest (i.e. the cost to the bank of the loan). This means that monthly payments are significantly lower but that no money is going towards paying off the mortgage. At the end of the mortgage term, the amount borrowed is due in full, in one go.

This type of repayment plan is usually used by investors who are looking to optimise their rental income, as the monthly cost is cheaper and over time the property should steadily increase in value.

Choose carefully

When choosing the correct type of mortgage for you, there really is no right or wrong. It's all about personal preference and your personal situation. If you want monthly security, then a fixed-term mortgage might work; but if you want a low mortgage now and have no desire to pay it off, then an interest-only mortgage might suit you better.

However, all of the aforementioned mortgage and repayment styles have one thing common — and that is the hefty penalty attached for breaking the deal before the fixed term ends. For example, if you win the lottery three months into your mortgage deal and you pay it off, you will have a fine to pay. This can run into thousands, depending on the value of the property, as the cost of this penalty is usually a percentage of the mortgage. This is something to consider when purchasing.

It's important to choose the right deal for your circumstances, as it would be awful to waste a large amount of money because you've decided to sell before the mortgage term is over.

The deposit

As most of you will know, the deposit is the major expense when buying a residence. unless you're **a cash buyer**, you will always need a decent deposit to start you off.

The deposit is essentially a down payment towards your property. The bank is lending you thousands of pounds in the form of a mortgage, so they expect you to put something towards it — and that something is a deposit. Your mortgage is paid back with interest and in basic terms the higher deposit you put down, the lower the interest rate.

Example

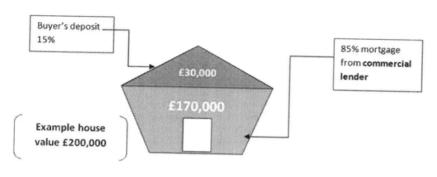

In the past, banks would give buyers 100% mortgages. This meant that as long as people were able to meet their monthly repayments, they did not have to worry about putting down a deposit.

Unfortunately, this created problems within the market. As property values fell, mortgage rates went up. Homeowners couldn't afford to pay and defaulted on their mortgages, leading to a number of **repossessions.** When the banks seized these properties, most were worth less than the banks had lent initially in the form of 100% mortgages. This meant that the banks had less money than when they started, and could no longer lend out for new mortgages. In turn, a domino effect meant that they had less money to lend in other markets too. This is what ultimately led to the financial crisis of 2008.

As a result, banks are now much more cautious lenders which, sadly for buyers, means that it is much tougher to get a mortgage offer, and that larger deposits are needed.

To purchase a property on a standard residential mortgage you will need *at least* a 10% deposit (although 15% is more likely). For a buy-to let investment property you will need at least 25%. Therefore it's imperative that when planning to buy, you implement a robust saving strategy and that you keep the deposit amount in mind at all times.

Stamp duty

Stamp duty is essentially a tax on the full purchase price of your property, paid by the buyer. You do not have to pay VAT when buying a home, but the Government takes its cut via stamp duty. In the past the Government lobbied to reduce or change stamp duty: for example, in 2010 all first-time buyers were exempt from stamp duty to encourage fluidity in the market and stimulate the economy. Since then this situation has changed, and stamp duty is now back in effect. Rules regarding how much the Government is able to take are not easy to work out at first glance, so here is a simple breakdown.

Table 1: Property purchase price and stamp duty

Purchase price of property	Rate of stamp duty	Buy to let/additional home* stamp duty
£0–£125,000	0%	3%
£125,001–£250,000	2%	5%
£250,001–£925,000	5%	8%
£925,001–£1.5 million	10%	13%
More than £1.5 million	12%	15%

* Correct as of April 2016

Example

Say you purchase a house for £275,000. The stamp duty you would pay is:

0% on the first £125,000 = £0

2% on the next £125,000 = £2,500

5% on the final £25,000 = £1,250

£2,500 + £1,250 = £3,750 total stamp duty

If you are doing a buy to let or purchasing a second property while retaining the first, then you pay an additional 3% on top.

Solicitor's costs

A conveyance solicitor specialises in property acquisition: they take care of all of the legal aspects of purchasing a property. This includes things such as doing local authority searches to check if your property is in a flood risk area, or if there have been any previous environmental issues in the vicinity. They also confirm important aspects of the purchase such as how long the **lease** is, how much the **service charge** will be each month, and what part of the property you will legally own (i.e. shared walls and loft space).

A solicitor's main role is to ensure that you have all the legal facts of the property and to oversee the transferral of the property from the previous owner into your name. Solicitor's costs usually end up between £2,000 and £3,000, depending on which solicitor you use.

> **TIP: We recommend going on personal recommendation as a way to check out various firms. If that is not an option, shop around in the area where you will be buying. Local solicitors will have good knowledge of local laws and leases.**

Speak with at least three to five solicitors, using price point, service and local knowledge for comparison.

The survey

Every buyer should complete a professional survey once the sale on a property has commenced. This is your opportunity as the buyer to gain a full overview of the property. Within the survey, you will find out if there are any structural, electrical or plumbing problems. It also covers things you may not have noticed, such as pest infestation. Surveys are carried out by a Royal Institution of Chartered Surveyors (RICS) professional, and at the end of the inspection they will present you with a property report.

Some people worry that surveyors are biased. However, you are *their* client. If they've missed something vitally important with the property and it later presents a problem, they could be sued. Therefore, you tend to find that most surveyors are very thorough. This can be very off-putting to vendors, but it's extremely reassuring to buyers, because you know exactly what you are getting into.

There are three types of survey you can instruct.

Basic lender's valuation

This is the cheapest, costing around £250. This consists of a representative from your mortgage lender taking a look at the property to ensure that they agree with the sale price, so that they can protect their investment. They do not tell you anything that they've found, but it can be useful to have an objective eye on the current property price.

Homebuyer's report

This costs around £450, and is excellent for purpose-built flats and more modern properties. This service gives a full valuation, plus a breakdown of the condition of the property. It includes any signs of damage that needs repairing, except for the actual structure of the building, and will give you a good idea of any work that needs to be completed before you move in.

Full structural survey

This is the 'big daddy' of surveys, and costs between £600 and £1,000. This is extremely important if you are purchasing a house (as opposed to a new-build flat), as it looks for evidence of major issues such as **subsidence** and other matters which may be potentially unsafe.

Moving costs

These costs are often overlooked. Unlike rental properties, most purchased homes come with little to no amenities included, which means that you need to budget for things such as furniture (bed, wardrobe, sofa) and white goods (fridge, washing machine, etc.). In addition, you will have to consider any refurbishments or decoration: with a relatively new property, this could be as simple as wallpapering or painting. However, in older properties you may want (or need) to do more extensive work.

Other costs to consider include removal costs and a professional clean. (This isn't a necessity, but we found it useful to have a property we could move straight into without worrying about deep cleaning following building works – see Chapter 7: 'The End of Tenancy Clean'.)

Moving costs are completely flexible and vary from person to person. When we moved into our first property we chose to keep costs at a minimum. We bought our sofa and dining table from the vendor, and got the rest of our furniture from IKEA and the British Heart Foundation store.

There is no right or wrong amount to put aside for moving costs, so have a think about what you need – and make sure to get several quotes for services such as decoration, removals and cleaning.

The budget

We're sure many of you are shuddering in horror at the thought of saving the constituent parts for a house purchase. We often get asked how we managed to save up, and we can tell you that although it is a very difficult task, it is by no means impossible! There are a number of ways you can reduce your costs in order to build up a reasonable deposit.

Set your budget

The first thing you need to do is to work out *how much* you need to save. After factoring in these costs, you should have a workable figure. This varies from person to person depending on the cost of the property you hope to buy, and your current level of savings.

Get fiscally fit

We cannot stress how important this is. In Lildonia's work as a life coach, she comes across a number of people who are completely and utterly frazzled by the state of their financial affairs. It's easy to become overwrought with worry about how your cash will last you until the next payday, or to overspend month-to-month.

On a fundamental level, taking things back to basics should be your first step. Analyse all of your outgoings and income (we love the 'Spending Tracker' app, see Further Resources), and see where cutbacks can be made.

Example

Do you really need to buy a coffee every day?

Does your night out really need to cost so much, or could a 'bring your own' night in work just as well?

Do you really need that yoga studio or high-end gym membership?

You get the picture!

Our generation is encouraged to have it all — but let's face it, having it all comes at a price. There's room for restraint within most young professionals' weekly costs, so really get stuck in and make some cuts. There are loads of voucher sites to ensure you can still live well on a shoestring, and websites such as Money Saving Expert (www.moneysavingexpert.com) which can help you to shave unnecessary expenditure.

Another factor to consider is how and where you hold your savings. Once you've established how much you can save a month, set up a monthly standing order from your current account to your savings account (out of sight, out of mind!).

TIP: Schedule meetings with all of the high street banks, plus other smaller, lesser-known building societies, to compare rates on savings accounts and ISAs. The internet is a great comparison tool for this.

If you're struggling with debt repayments, it's essential to get those cleared as soon as possible. We're not financial experts, but there are a lot of people out there who are. Consider seeing a professional financial planner or debt adviser who can support you to create a savings plan and get a hold of your finances. Even though dealing with money can be stressful, it's even more stressful to bury your head in the sand and allow problems to mount up.

Go for gold

Have a think about your current working situation. Are you living up to your earning potential? If you're a long way away from your final financial goal, it may be time to consider your career path alongside your home-owning path. Perhaps it's the time to go for a promotion or raise at work? Maybe it's time to look for a higher paid role altogether! For example, we have friends who work two or three jobs in order to save, do weekend work or work in family businesses.

Think about your hobbies. Could any of them work as a sideline for you? Lildonia once had a particularly tenacious client who worked as a mobile hairdresser alongside her full-time work as a nurse.

Think about your skills too. There are a number of websites such as Fiverr (www.fiverr.com) which allow you to sell your offer online, from editing to graphic design. Get creative, think outside the box and discover the new places that your skill set could take you. Of course, work–life balance is important, and we are by no means suggesting you kill yourself or sell your soul in order to raise funds, but we are suggesting you review your current income situation, to maximise your earning potential.

Ask around

Share your goal with friends and family. Most will want to support you and will be pleased to see you working towards something. Ask your circle to forgo holiday and birthday presents, and ask them to transfer the cash into your savings account instead. Ok, it's not as cute as the carefully chosen presents of yesteryear, but it will be pretty sweet when you see the figures racking up in your account!

There is no shame in this: many people will be relieved that they're getting you something you actually want, and parents or family members may offer to contribute a lot to your house fund. Just make sure to keep it locked away, and resist the temptation to treat yourself with the money.

Share your abode

Private rental prices, particularly in London and the South-East, are ridiculously high. Many areas which were seen previously as 'no-go' areas have been gentrified, becoming trendy hotspots. This has pushed rental prices up, and now these neighbourhoods have gone from unaffordable to astronomical. For example, in many parts of London, and in Oxford and Cambridge, you would be hard-pushed to find a one-bedroom flat for anything less than £1,000pcm! The chances are you will be paying much more if you choose a central location in a city. This means that private renting is becoming more of a luxury than a necessity for most.

Flatsharing

Both of us come across clients in our respective industries of young career types enjoying city life in expensive and fashionable areas, while complaining about property prices and grumbling that they'll have to rent forever. We always encourage the same thing: wherever possible, get yourself a flatshare!

With the rise of websites such as Spare Room (www.spareroom.com), it's easier than ever to find flatmates. For example, splitting the cost of a

£2,500pcm four-bedroom flat is a lot easier to manage, and hopefully will give you a bit more wriggle room when it comes to saving.

Along with considering *who* you are sharing with, make sure to think about *where* you live. City centre apartments are not essential, and if you can find somewhere within a one-hour radius of your work but outside the major locations of your region, the chances are it will be a lot cheaper to rent.

Subletting

If you have the space, are willing (and allowed), you could always consider taking in a lodger. Many people we know rent a two-bedroom flat with the vague idea of hosting friends and family that never come around often enough to make it worthwhile. Of course, this is dependent on whether your landlord is happy for you to share the property and sublet part of the space. If they are, it could be a great way to earn extra cash on the side and get some help towards every day bills.

Living at home

Another option for sharing could be with your parents. Yes, we know it may be the last thing you want, but a growing number of working adults are returning home due to high rental prices and property purchase being out of reach. It's not uncommon to see 30 to-35-year-olds with good jobs and salaries leaving the office at the end of the day to a lovely home-cooked meal with mum and dad. There is absolutely no shame in this.

After leaving our first rat-infested home (which we mentioned in the Introduction), we moved in with Lildonia's mum for a year in order to save up for our first deposit. Had we not had that opportunity, it would have been a lot harder to buy.

If this option is available to you, speak with your parents and ask if you can pay as little as possible towards housekeeping in return for a promise to lock away a large chunk of your salary towards your deposit. Your parents will feel safe in the knowledge that: (a) they're supporting you on the way to your first home; and (b) you won't be there forever!

If you are living at home, make sure you set out tangible saving goals, as sometimes it is easy to forget about the end goal and enjoy lower outgoings a bit too much. With easy access to travel, meals out and club nights, it's easy to get caught up in life, frittering away any potential savings made by living back with family.

Many people living at home in their twenties and thirties are having the time of their lives holidaying, partying and having a general knees-up. That's fantastic for them, but if this is about a property you want, these activities may have to go by the wayside for a while.

It's all about priorities – besides, you'll be able to host a ton of house parties when you get your own pad!

Stay on track

This is the most important point of all. As we reinforced in the previous chapter, sticking to your goal is imperative. View your savings as money you don't even own, and stand firm against the appeal of easily accessible cash in your account.

We met a couple last year who had been saving for three years for a property due to their rental flat being too small to start a family. During that time, the boyfriend proposed, and the couple proceeded to spend £10,000 of their savings on a wedding and £3,000 on a honeymoon.

Granted, this isn't a lot in the scheme of weddings – but they'd blown a large proportion of their savings and had to start from scratch as soon as the wedding was over. Both say that if they could, they either would have had a much cheaper wedding, or held off on getting married until they had purchased their flat.

Now they are stuck with a pricey but small flat, and finding it difficult to save up for the future.

We urge you all to remember your goal along the way. When you are faltering and feel slightly jealous of friends' endless nights out or trips away, just think about why you are working towards a property – and what it would mean to you to own your own home.

My Budget

_____

_____

_____

_____

_____

_____

_____

_____

_____

_____

My Costs

Item	Estimated cost	Actual cost
Deposit		
Stamp duty		
Solicitor's costs		
Survey costs		
Moving costs		
Other costs		

Conclusion

As you can see, there are a number of economic aspects to consider on the journey to procurement, and saving up is a massive part of the house-buying process. It's not fun, it's not pretty, but it's seriously important – and it will be more then worth it in the long run. Take this time to have a think about how you can get your finances in order, and set a budget for your individual property needs.

Notes

Chapter 3

●   ●   ●

Government Schemes and How to Use Them

There is a lot of talk about these schemes at the moment, and this is something we are asked about frequently. People question whether they are good or bad, and what on earth these proposals mean!

This chapter will cover the current schemes available as of the financial year 2016/17. If you decide to use a government scheme, it's important to do your research as things change quickly, and new schemes often come up.

There are four main government schemes currently being offered to first-time buyers:

1.   Shared Ownership Scheme
2.   Help to Buy
3.   Help to Buy: Mortgage Guarantee
4.   Help to Buy ISA.

Shared Ownership Scheme

This can be quite a confusing road to take, as there are a lot of mixed opinions regarding whether this format is beneficial or not. Often, traditional homeowners (our parents' generation) are anti-shared ownership, and discourage their children from using it.

When we first discussed the idea of using shared ownership as a means to buy, Lildonia's mum said: 'I'm not sure it's a good idea. Just think about the name... a scheme isn't called a scheme for nothing!' However, despite what people may think, shared ownership does work well for many – and it is the format we used when we purchased our first property.

How it works

In a nutshell, buying through shared ownership means purchasing part of a property from a housing association. One segment you own, and the other you rent. The halves are not always equal, so you may be able to buy 25% of your home and pay rent on 75% or you may split the cost 50/50. You pay a monthly mortgage to your lender and monthly rental costs will be at predetermined amount set by the housing association.

Once you own this segment, however small, you are usually responsible for all of the upkeep and maintenance of the property, despite only being a partial owner. The benefit of using shared ownership is that you only have to raise capital and receive a mortgage offer for the share of the property you are buying.

> **Example**
> You are buying a £100,000 property. If you put in 50%, you will only need to get a deposit and mortgage for £50,000.

Shared ownership schemes are also a handy way of buying property in notoriously unaffordable areas. For many, this method is a much more affordable way of getting on the property ladder.

There is also room for investment potential using this scheme. If your property value increases, so does the share that you own – meaning you will have built equity on your half. That equity is yours to keep, which gives you the possibility for a cash injection when you sell or remortgage. If you remortgage with a higher level of equity than you started with, you will have more capital stored within the half that you own. Alternatively, if you sell, you can use this extra cash as a deposit for a new property.

> **TIP: Most shared ownership properties are exempt from being rental properties until you fully own them. This means that if you purchase these properties, you must intend to live in them.**
> **The rules are different in Northern Ireland, Scotland and Wales, so contact your local authority to find out about shared ownership in your area.**

Who is eligible?

You can buy your home through shared ownership if your household earns £80,000 a year or less (£90,000 or less in London), and any of the following apply:

* You're a first-time buyer
* You used to own a home but cannot afford to buy one presently
* You're an existing shared owner of a property.

Things to consider

You can buy more shares of your home as time progresses: this is known as **staircasing**. The cost of your new shares will depend on how much your home is worth when you want to buy more. If property prices in your area have gone up, it will cost more, and vice versa. The housing association will provide an independent valuation of your property, and inform you of the cost of your new share. You also will have to pay a valuation fee, which is usually around £400.

If you want to sell your share of the property, the housing association has the right to buy it first: this is known as **first refusal**. It also has the right to find a buyer on your behalf. Conversely, if you own 100% of your home, you can sell it yourself on the open market with no say from the housing association.

The main thing to remember is that the goal of purchasing via shared ownership is not necessarily to eventually own the entire property. For lots of people, it is a step in the right direction to increase equity for a future purchase. For example, 100% ownership of a £100,000 property is the same as 50% of a £200,000 property: it's not how much of a percentage you *own*, but how much that percentage is *actually worth*.

Help to Buy scheme

The Help to Buy scheme is an **equity loan**. This means that the Government puts in a proportion of the purchase price of a property, to help people buy one with a lower deposit.

How it works

As a buyer, you put up a 5% deposit of the total property price, and the Government *lends* you up to 20% on top (40% in London). To participate in this format, you need a mortgage to cover the other 75% (55% in London).

The main appeal of this is that the buyer can save up a smaller deposit for their ideal property. The rate they will pay on their mortgage is also lower, as their total deposit will be higher than it would be without the government loan, meaning lower interest rates. This allows people to buy a property that they would not otherwise have been able to afford – albeit with the assistance of the chaps in Westminster.

Who is eligible?

Anyone – however, the home you purchase must:

* be new build from a registered developer within the scheme
* have a purchase price of up to £600,00 (£300,000 in Wales)
* be the only property you own
* not be sublet or rented out.

Things to consider

Remember, the key is in the name: equity *loan*. The Government is not granting you this cash, simply loaning the sum to you for its own return on investment. This happens to be mutually beneficial for both parties, but it is important to remember the dynamic. However much the property increases in value, the Government is still due back its percentage of 40%. This means the Government stands to profit greatly from this venture, in proportion to how much it invested at the start.

There are also equity loan fees that will need to be paid back. They start in the sixth year after purchase, and are charged at 1.75% of the loan's value. This fee then increases every year according to the **Retail Price Index** plus 1%. You get a statement about your loan annually, which is set up with your Home Buy officer (sadly these fees don't count towards paying back your loan).

You will need to pay back your loan after 25 years, or whenever you sell your property (whichever comes first). The amount you pay back depends on how much your home is worth (i.e. its current market value).

Fundamentally, the Government is using the previously mentioned notion of leverage to its own advantage. So, once the property is sold, you get back your 5% (a figure that includes any equity accumulated), and the Government gets back its 40% invested. The rest of the cash earned goes to paying off the outstanding mortgage.

Some argue that this is not a fair system, as the Government benefits highly from the equity built up on a property where the individual is paying the monthly mortgage. However, it is important to remember that buyers using the Help to Buy scheme wouldn't have been able to purchase a property without it. As the property owner, you are also building equity within the proportion to which you have invested, just as the Government is.

It's no small accomplishment to live in a new brand new flat in a decent area – which is what the Help to Buy scheme offers. Although people on this scheme find it hard to build a large amount of equity by using this method, it can be a good option for people who are simply looking forward to having a brand spanking new home for the foreseeable future.

Help to Buy: Mortgage Guarantee

This is another government scheme which allows you to buy a home with a much smaller than average deposit of 5% or 10%. It is similar to the common practice of tenants using a guarantor on a tenancy agreement to provide landlord security, by legally binding a third party to the agreement.

With a mortgage guarantee, the lender runs a financial assessment on you as the buyer to ensure you can make the repayments; however, it does so with the understanding that the Government will be acting as your guarantor.

How it works

This scheme does exactly what it says on the tin: if you default on your mortgage, the Government will act as your warm and snugly guarantor by ensuring that the lender has an 'indemnity' to cover any losses that result from the default.

This supports lenders to feel safe in the knowledge that their investment will be protected, and allows them to offer you a higher loan to value (LTV) mortgage (albeit with a higher interest rate). To apply for this scheme you contact your lender and they will complete the process with you.

> **TIP: This format is handy for professionals who have high wages (which allows for higher mortgage repayments), but do not have a deposit saved up proportional to the property price.**

Example

If you earn £100,000 a year, in theory you could be eligible for a mortgage of up to £500,000. That sounds great, but 15% on a £500,000 property is still a whopping £75,000 without factoring stamp duty and moving costs.

Even someone on a £100,000 salary, with no external financial help, will struggle to save this amount in any viable time frame – especially in urban hubs around the country.

This scheme makes purchasing higher-priced property much more attainable for high earners, and frees up the lower end of the market to more 'average earners'. This keeps higher earners out of the low to mid-priced first-time buyer market, and in theory removes demand in this arena, keeping prices from inflating too rapidly.

Another positive of this scheme is that the individual gets to keep all of the equity that has been acquired over time, and the Government does not have any stake in the property.

Who is eligible?

Anyone – however, the home you buy must:

* have a purchase price of £600,000 or less
* be the only home you own
* not be rented out after purchase
* not be bought through any other publicly-funded mortgage scheme
* be bought on a repayment (as opposed to an interest-only) mortgage.

Things to consider

There is not much to think about, bar the higher interest rates on these type of mortgages. There are also fewer lenders out there who are willing to offer this scheme, which may restrict the amount of lenders you can approach, which in turn might restrict your choice of mortgage deal.

Having said that, there aren't many choices of lender at a 95% LTV rate anyway, so the cons are not much of a negative at all!

Help to Buy ISA

If you're saving to buy your first home, the Government will top up your savings by 25% (up to £3,000). If you're purchasing with someone else, they can use this ISA too.

How it works

Your first ISA payment can be up to £1,200, then you can pay in £200 a month. When you come to buy your property, your solicitor will apply for the extra 25% from the Government. It's a fantastic way to help to save that bit extra on top of your deposit.

Who is eligible?

First-time buyers – the home you buy must:

* have a purchase price of up to £250,000 (£450,000 in London)
* be the only home you own
* be where you intend to live.

Things to consider

Not much! The best thing about this scheme is that you don't have to pay it back. It's *free money*, and who doesn't like that?

Conclusion

As you can see, there are a number of potential schemes out there at your disposal. It's important to conduct your own research into this area when considering buying a property – as we mentioned at the start of this chapter, these schemes are updated and revised often.

Friends and family may have strong opinions on this topic, which might impact on how you feel about each option. The most important thing is to evaluate the *facts*, rather than simply listening to a relative or friend who may have bought their home in a completely different era to where we are now.

When deciding which scheme to use, please also bear in mind your *final goal*. There is no point of opting for a scheme that doesn't align with your ultimate purpose, as you could end up stuck in a bad situation.

Consider all your options, discuss with your mortgage adviser, and think carefully before you make your final decision.

Notes

Chapter 4

●　　●　　●

The 'Ideal Property' Plan

So, you've created your budget, saved your deposit and secured your mortgage in principle. Great! Now it's time to get down to the most important bit: finding the right property.

Before you even start looking, it's important to clarify what you want and why.

When we bought our first flat, we were very clear. We wanted a one-bedroom, newish flat with good access to a train station, reasonable proximity to both of our jobs, within 45 minutes' travel distance to our family and friends. Luckily, we were able to find a property that fit those specifications, and we lived there happily for four years.

Our second property wasn't quite as straightforward: we didn't nail down exactly what we were looking for, or our overall goal. The result was that we ended up in a very good investment property, but not a property that suited us or our current situation.

There is absolutely no point blindly viewing hundreds of properties and hoping that one will magically jump out at you. It won't! The first thing you need is to create an outline of your ideal property, so that you will know when you've found it.

There is an enormous range of properties out there, and each style will have its benefits and pitfalls. As part of creating your ideal property plan, it's important to understand the different types.

Before we get started, let's go through some of the key terms that you will need to know on your property journey.

Learn the lingo

Freehold

This is a type of ownership in the UK mainly associated with houses. Having a freehold of the property means that you own the house in its entirety. This includes the structural walls, roof, foundations and interior. It also covers the land on which the property sits, meaning that any changes you want to make the property usually can be done, subject to planning permission with the local council. This could be alterations such as extensions and loft conversions.

Leasehold

A leasehold property in the UK is mainly associated with flats. This means that in essence you are simply embarking on a very long tenancy. During this 'tenancy' you purchase the 'ownership' from the freeholder for a fixed period of time. A 'new' lease often starts at between 99 and 1,000 years, and decreases with the passing of time (e.g. a property with a 90-year lease).

With a leasehold property you 'own' the interior dwelling, but neither the physical structure of the building, nor the land that it sits on – this means you are unable to make structural changes such as extensions. This is because most leasehold properties will share the same land and structure as other apartments within one building, and so any changes to one part of it will have an effect on the others.

The freeholder owns the physical building, and there will be an identical **head lease** between themselves and each of the leaseholders, which both parties must follow. All communal areas such as stairways, roofs, brickwork, structures and hallways are the freeholder's responsibility: it's their job to make sure these are maintained to a decent standard.

As a covenant of the head lease, a service charge is usually payable to the freeholder each month. The freeholder could be an individual, developer, property management company or the local council.

Service charge

This is a monthly or annual fee that the leaseholder pays to the freeholder for upkeep of all the communal areas. Most likely it will include buildings insurance, meaning that the freeholder (and you as the leaseholder) are covered, should there be any major issues with the building. This cost can vary between £50 and £1,000 a month, depending on the type of development.

The more services provided by the freeholder, the higher the service charge. So, if you move into a development with a gym, swimming pool and porter, you will have a high service charge. However, most standard flats are around £60 to £150 a month.

Ground rent

This is another monthly or annual cost to factor in as a leaseholder. It's a price paid from the leaseholder to the freeholder for the right occupy the physical land on which the property stands. It is separate from the service charge, but it's often grouped together with the charge as a monthly or annual payment.

Share of freehold

This is a mixture between freehold and leasehold, and often present in small developments of flats as a part of one larger converted house. It means that along with their lease, each owner of the flats has a share in the ownership of the freehold. This means that any decisions made about the development are made by joint agreement of all the shared freeholders, including how service charges are spent.

In share of freehold, responsibility for the structure of the building is shared between all the property owners.

Development

This is a group of properties which may include **commercial units**. Usually, it has been planned out in conjunction with the local authority.

Conversion

This is a building which was originally a house, then converted to flats at a later date.

Purpose-built

This is a group of flats built specifically as residential dwellings, and not for any other use.

Ex-local authority (ex-council)

This is a property previously owned by the council, but now privately owned. Often, the Council is still the freeholder.

National House Building Council (NHBC) 10-year warranty

Nearly all newly-built homes come with a NHBC 10-year labour guarantee from the developer. If any issues develop, you don't necessarily need to pay for repairs, as the warranty will cover them.

Types of properties

So now you've got the lingo down, it's time to get your head around the different types of property. As always, when considering what type of home to buy, *keep the final destination in mind*. If you are looking for a family home, there is probably no point buying a super-swanky penthouse apartment with three flights of stairs and no lift!

Houses

A house is generally a building consisting of a ground floor and one or more upper levels. It's a standalone residential structure, and usually freehold with no ongoing service charges or head lease to be concerned about.

Pros:

* Often has a garden
* Can be developed and extended into the garden or loft (subject to planning permission)
* Traditional living style
* Low ongoing costs with no service charge or ground rent
* Fewer neighbours compared to apartment living
* No shared communal space
* May have additional features such as a driveway or garage.

Cons:

* You are responsible for the entire structure of the building as well as any walls, fences or outside space that make up the property
* Needs buildings insurance, which may be costly depending on the building
* Higher priced then apartments and flats.

Types of houses

There are plethora of house styles, depending on the area where you live and the period when they were built. We'll be going over the main types of house you are likely to come across.

Detached

A detached house is one which is not connected to any other building on all four sides. This is the dream for many homeowners, and is seen as the holy grail of comfortable living for lots of people. These are very expensive, and rare within cities. You'll find that these houses are mainly found outside of the city centre and owned by footballers, minor celebrities, high-earning CEOs (you catch our drift!). They are at a premium in urban areas, as fewer are being built in favour of higher-density units. You are more likely to find a reasonably priced detached house in the suburbs and rural areas.

Semi-detached

This is a house connected to one house on the end side. Each house is often a mirror image of the other, both internally and externally. These properties have been built throughout a number of eras, but are synonymous with post-war city suburbs.

According to a Nationwide report of July 2010, in the UK semi-detached houses are the most common property type, accounting for 32% of all UK housing stock. Between 1945 and 1964, 41% of all properties built were semis, but after 1980 this fell to just 15%, showing a shift toward the building of flats. After the Second World War, many of the UK's inner cities became run down following the bombing, and so houses were built on the outskirts of town in this style to accommodate growing demand. These houses are still deemed very desirable by many people today.

Terraced

A terraced house is one where multiple houses are connected on both sides in a row. The houses in the middle are call mid-terrace, and the ones at the end of the row are called end-of-terrace.

End-of-terrace properties are usually more desirable, as they give a semi-detached feel without the higher semi-detached price tag. They usually hail from the Victorian era, and are found most often near city centres. In the Victorian period, terraced houses were built near factories and railways to house workers. Although many of the factories have now disappeared, the houses still remain.

Often, terraced houses are not very big, but they appear in excellent central locations and can be extended to create additional space. Modern-day developers frequently use this layout, as it is both space and cost-effective when building a large number of houses simultaneously.

Townhouse

This is a modern style of terraced house first introduced in the 1970s. Generally, townhouses will have the functionality of a house with a driveway or garage, but with a more unique layout and smaller physical footprint.

Typically, townhouses are spread over three or more floors, with a kitchen/ dining room on the ground, a reception room and bedroom on the first floor, and a bathroom and two further bedrooms on the second. Sometimes they can feel narrow, as the square footage is spread vertically over a number of floors, but they do offer all the main benefits of a house. Something to be aware of is that many modern townhouses are part of a wider development, and so may have a head lease and service charge.

Mews house

Traditionally, a mews house is a converted private stable. In the 17th and 18th centuries, the large homes of the gentry had stables to house their horses; over time, many of these stables were destroyed and redeveloped, as the need for horses declined. There are a few that have survived and been converted into small and quirky homes. Mews houses are often situated around a central communal courtyard located between rows of adjacent houses. This can provide for a lovely community feel for those living there.

Due to these houses' previous usage, the living space is not always efficient. It is extremely condensed, and some people describe mews properties as feeling hemmed in. These types of properties tend to be freehold, high in price and hold a high value in the open market.

Apartments

Now it's time to move on to apartments, a large aspect of modern living. Cities and towns have grown larger in size since the late 19th century and, as a result, living space has come at a premium. In order to provide maximum economic growth, town planners aimed to house as many people as possible close to central hubs and city centres. This became ever more difficult, as the population rose and as more people moved from rural locations to embark on inner-city and town living.

As a result, the number of apartments being built has grown extensively since the early 1900s. Nowadays, apartments are commonplace, and most people will live in one at some point during their lives.

There are two main types of flats:

* purpose-built apartments, which were specifically designed as individual residential units
* conversions from buildings with a prior use.

Purpose-built apartments

Victorian, Edwardian or period mansion block

These blocks are usually found close to stations and community hubs, often within city centres. They were built following the terraced house era as a way to fit multiple people into a lateral space, while keeping a high calibre of decor for the emerging middle classes of the time.

Pros:

*   A lot of internal and external character and original features (cast-iron fireplaces, decorative detailing)
*   Spacious interior rooms – a two-bedroom flat easily can be 1,000 square feet as standard

* Lots of natural light from multiple large windows
* Functional and practical layout, with large square rooms
* Often with high ceilings
* Sometimes have the use of a private balcony
* Often come with communal gardens.

Cons:

* Usually higher priced then other purpose-built apartments due to the many plus points
* High service charges for often grand and large gardens
* Many neighbours above, below and either side
* Often no parking due to many flats within close proximity
* Pets are not usually allowed.

Art Deco mansion block

These blocks were built in the 1920s and 1930s. Although they serve the same purpose as the previous period, they are styled completely differently. They have a very striking style and often appear geometrically symmetrical, with architectural straight lines. The emphasis within the design of an art deco mansion block is on form and function.

Pros:

* Found in central locations
* Generous size in terms of total square footage
* Sometimes have a porter
* Communal gardens are common
* Functional living space with square or rectangle rooms and doors and windows strategically placed
* Cheaper compared to other types of property on the market.

Cons:

* External architecture is not as stylish as other types of mansion block
* Pets are not usually allowed
* Often a high service charge attached
* A low chance of off-street parking due to central locations.

Tower block: 1960s high-rise

These were built in the years following the Second World War, and as a result were all about rejuvenation and serving a need for housing quickly and efficiently for those who had lost their homes during the war. Typically, this type of high rise is constructed from interconnecting slabs of concrete, often visually exposed to demonstrate the structural stability and security that comes from the relatively 'new' material.

Many were built in city centres, and can now be found in most towns and cities throughout the UK. They are usually individual blocks or part of larger estates. Many were built for the local authority, and remain council-owned today.

Pros:

* Often found in central locations
* Often have a functional and fit-for-purpose living space
* Usually much cheaper to buy then other types (particularly if they are ex-council)
* Concrete provides excellent soundproofing between flats
* Often comes with allocated or underground parking
* Great views from the higher floors.

Cons:

* Many of the buildings are now considered an eyesore
* Have statistically higher levels of antisocial behaviour
* Many flats within one unit, and as a result lots of unknown people coming and going on the estate
* Hard to get a mortgage above the second floor
* If the local council is still the freeholder, can be slower and less responsive than private management agents to fix communal issues.
* At the time of writing, there have been concerns around the fire safety of these blocks, following the tragedy of Grenfell Tower in west London in 2017.

Apartment block: 1980s and 1990s low-rise

Due to the fact that most people developed strong negative feelings towards the 1960s blocks, private developers began to take changing tastes of society into account. This led to blocks with similar functionality to the 1960s high rises, but with a more individualistic exterior.

As space became more of a premium, property sizes began to reduce, meaning that sometimes the flats within these blocks can be small in size. Decor-wise, they are usually very bland, with no features to write home about. One interesting aspect of these flats is that gas central heating is not always guaranteed for properties within these type of blocks, and often outdated storage heaters are used.

Pros:

* 1980s and 1990s blocks are easier on the eye then blocks from previous periods

* Layout is often functional, meaning that furniture fits well inside them
* Service charges are usually reasonably priced
* The ideal blank canvas to modernise internally.

Cons:

* Quite generic and lacking in character
* Size can be an issue, as usually they are smaller than 1960s blocks
* Interior walls can be made from plasterboard, giving the flats a somewhat flimsy feel – this can make it hard to hang heavy pictures or walls without additional support
* Often have small windows which leads to less light throughout.

New-builds

These properties are what everyone has been talking about, and are seen as the hot ticket for young professionals. They began to spring up towards the end of the 2000s, after the 2008 financial crash. Developers saw a big opportunity, and began buying disused land in central locations to convert into new-build developments. These developments consist of flats, sometimes houses and often retail units. They have no real style guide, and can really differ externally from development to development.

These flats are designed for modern life, and are geared towards young professionals or the young family. They can pop up in up-and-coming or newly-gentrified areas, and visual styles can vary wildly. There might be huge, sprawling metropolis-style developments, or smaller ones with only a few blocks. The internal specifications of these properties can vary, ranging from a standard outfit (ceramic tiles, laminate floor, etc.) to top-of-the-range design (granite worktops, air conditioning, controlled lighting, etc.)

Pros:

* Often built in strategically placed and convenient locations with good transport links
* Either brand new or recently built
* Good energy efficiency means lower bills
* Sometimes come with other features such as a gym, pool, porter or underground parking
* Retail units and convenience stores often built within the development
* Visually pleasing to modern tastes
* Come with a NHBC 10-year warranty – no worries about old, leaky pipes and roofs caving in

* When purchased brand new, developers may throw in extras such as furniture and white goods
* Many come with a balcony.

Cons:

* Can be quite tight on space
* Service charges can be quite high – especially if there are extra amenities such as a concierge, fitness suite, etc.
* Some people feel that the properties have a 'halls of residence' feel, due to many flats situated off one long corridor
* Often developments have many flats in a small space, which can lead to congestion and traffic build-up in the local area
* New builds can be the first to depreciate in a period of economic downturn
* If there is no car park, chances are you will not be able to get a permit from the council – due to council restrictions when allowing the developer the right to build
* Many flats may face directly onto others, leading to a lack of privacy
* Often lack any local character – new builds all over the world tend to have a similar style.

Conversions

Conversions are properties which have been converted from their original usage as a large house into two or more flats. There are conversions from different periods. For example, a Victorian conversion describes flats created from a Victorian-period house. Most conversions will retain some of the features of the original house, but this is not always a given.

Pros:

* Can look quite homely from the outside, depending on the period in which they were built
* Often have a unique and interesting layout
* Top-floor flats with a loft may be converted (subject to planning permission)
* Ground-floor conversions often come with parking and/or a garden.

Cons:

* Can be noisy due to lack of concrete between floors – neighbours are more likely to hear each other's daily movements
* Can be pricey, as people are willing to pay more for a converted property
* Not purpose-built, so can have odd-shaped rooms
* Usually smaller, as the total square footage is less efficiently used in comparison to a purpose-built block.

Your features list

Now that you've analysed the different types of properties, you should be starting to get an idea of the style of home you like. Of course, the design of the house is not the only issue to consider – there are a number of other factors which need to be given careful contemplation.

Location

This is one of the biggest clichés out there, but the physical locality of a property makes a massive difference.

Location is a really important piece of the puzzle for many people. Some people want to be close to friends and family, while others need a buzzy town centre and good transport links. Everyone is different, so it's vital to think about what's important to you. Remember: compromises will need to be made.

> **TIP: Properties far from local amenities will be cheaper and better value for money than properties in a popular location. For example, you can get a three-bedroom terraced property in suburban London for the same price as a one-bedroom flat in the inner city.**

Price

Regardless of how much you earn or how large a deposit you have, price will always come into it. Property can be infinitely expensive, and all buyers will have a maximum budget. When it comes to considering price, the main goal is to achieve the objectives of the purchase while sticking to your financial plan.

Size

This is a pretty self-explanatory: how big is the property? UK residences are measured in square feet. The higher the square feet, the larger the property. Floor plans are ideal for looking into this, but it's important to take the layout into consideration.

> **TIP: An $800sq^2$ conversion with stairs and a large internal corridor will seem a lot smaller than an $800sq^2$ flat with no corridor or staircase.**

Specification

Specification is all about the quality and finish of the furnishings within the property. Some vendors have kitted their property out with real solid wood floors and granite worktops, while others have used laminate flooring and chipboard.

Consider if this is important to you or not. Some people want a property that they can move into straightaway, while others want a renovation project. Similarly, some people want to enjoy a high-quality finish, while others are happy with more basic options. Included in this area may be benefits such as large windows and amount of natural light.

Features

Features are often promoted in estate agency details: they give the property the 'X-factor' and '**kerb appeal**'. Features that people tend to consider include their own front door, loft, garage, storage and outdoor space. This also can include what type of property it is: for example, whether you want a three-bed semi-detached house, or a new-build apartment.

It is super-important to analyse these five factors, and decide which are the most important to you and why. This also needs to marry up with your SMART goal and your intention behind buying a property in the first place. There is no point of looking for a large house in a nice area but far from amenities, if you are hoping to rent it out to young professionals who would prefer a flat in a more central location. Once you've had a think about all of this, it's time to design your ideal property and fill in your property star!

The Property Star

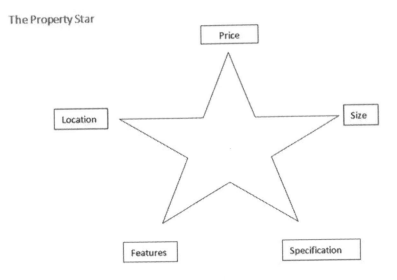

Each tip on the star is worth 10 points. Mark the properties you see out of 10, depending on how highly you feel they score: where 1 = awful and 10 = perfect. The ideal score will be 50 out of 50.

However, that is highly unlikely to happen, as a large property with a great location is likely to be high in price. Similarly, a low-priced property may not have great features or specifications. So, it's all about deciding what is most important to you.

Your first step is to put the factors of the property star in order of importance. Let's use our SMART goal from Chapter 1 to demonstrate.

Example

> I want to buy a two-bedroom property within the Greater Manchester Area, intending to rent out a room.
>
> This property will be my home for the medium-term future (5–10 years).
>
> I want to have purchased this property by August 20XX.

1. **Location** – This buyer specifically wants a property in the Greater Manchester Area.
2. **Price** – This buyer wants to use this property partially as a rental investment. This means the lower the price, the better.
3. **Size** – This person intends to share their property, meaning they need enough space for two adults to live comfortably.
4. **Specification** – This buyer does not care too much about specification, as it is not a 'forever home'. Good enough will do the job.
5. **Features** – This buyer is flexible in the features of the property, as long as it has two bedrooms.

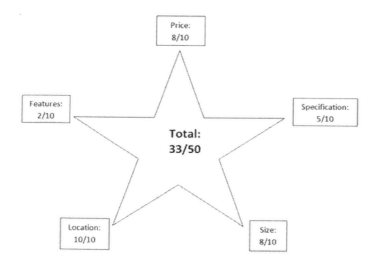

Once you've ordered your features list, you will have a better idea of how your personal property star should add up. This person's ideal property star would look something like this:

So although 33/50 doesn't seem like a great score, for this person it is because their top three factors (location, size and price) rank highly.

The aim is to create your 'ideal' star as a basis, then create a property star for each one you view (or serious contender), and see how they match up. The more willing you are to compromise, the better bargain you will get.

> **TIP: If specification is important to you but your budget does not allow for this, look to compromise on the specification factor and search for a renovation project.**
> **If size is important for the future but not necessary right now, you can reduce the importance of size, but look for a property with space to extend.**

For many young professionals, living in a buzzy location is an important factor – but that is definitely something which can be compromised on in order to save money. Instead, you could look at up-and-coming areas which are in the process of regeneration, meaning that the location will improve, the longer you live there.

Our first property was in relatively unknown area. The flat was next to a notoriously troubled estate, and there were no local shops, cafes, and so forth.

However, the one thing the area did possess was a train station with easy access to central London, and a large amount of open space. Over a period of four to five years the area transformed completely, and now includes numerous housing developments, supermarkets, pubs and restaurants, making it a fantastic location in which to live.

Conclusion

Please remember that there is no such thing as a 'perfect' property. If that is what you are looking for, then you will be searching a long time. Consider your options, and always think of the compromises. It you want an A-grade 50/50 super pad, you'll need the money to pay for it!

We hope this will help you to identify what features are important to you, and that you will gain a focal point when starting your property search. Once you have that laser-sharp focus, you will be well on your way to finding your (nearly) perfect home!

Notes

Chapter 5

●　●　●

The Property Search

If you've followed all of our steps so far, you should have an understanding of your budget, your chosen scheme (if you are using one), and the type of property that you are looking for.

Now it's time to move on to the exciting part of the journey: the property search! Although this is an exhilarating period, the search can be confusing, and it's easy to lose sight of what this process is all about. This chapter will guide you on how to make the most of your viewings, and how to use your time efficiently.

Dealing with estate agents

A major (yet often overlooked) part of your property search will be communication with sales agents. The estate agent is hired by the vendor to market (and eventually sell) their property, which they do for a fee. The fee is paid by the vendor once the property is sold, and the process has completed. If there is no sale, the agent does not receive any payment. Buying a property through an estate agent is completely free, and there are no fees involved for the buyer.

As the agent works primarily for the vendor as opposed to the buyer, they will do whatever they can to sell the property to whomever they can (within legal remit, of course!). Having said that, working well with the right agents can benefit you and your search immensely. Good relationships with estate agents can mean the difference between finding your dream home, and fruitless wandering in the property landscape.

Make sure to get on board with a few agents in the area: if you're in their good books, often they will make sure that you get the best market information, and a first look at the best properties.

Avoiding the hard sell

Many people find estate agents extremely annoying and hard to work with – we can completely understand, and Cory will be the first to admit that some agents let the side down in what is actually a very reputable industry.

Many firms push agents to be energetic, enthusiastic and sell, sell, sell! This means that they can be keen to get you out on viewings but may rush you through the process, brushing off any questions or concerns you may have. Sometimes they can come across as pushy, encouraging you to view properties that you are not keen to see.

They may say things such as:

> I think you should offer on this, as it is top floor with excellent views! I know you are having a baby next week and there are a lot of stairs, but it's an excellent place and there are three other people interested. Shall I discuss X amount with the vendor? You won't get anything better in this market!

It's important to stick to your guns and focus on the type of property *you* want, as opposed to the property an agent may try to push on you.

TIP: A good agent will be a master at understanding your needs, and should select places based on what you have said you're looking for. They should be respectful, polite and have excellent market knowledge.

Setting up viewings

When searching for a property, it's really important to get the most out of your hunt in order to optimise your time and ensure you don't miss out on your dream home.

As you might know already, your first port of call will be online portals. The top two in the UK are Zoopla (www.zoopla.co.uk) and Rightmove (www.rightmove.co.uk), but there are a few others.

Rightmove tends to be viewed as the most popular for its ease of use and the amount of properties listed. Most estate agents will list their stock on a number of property portals as well as their own website. These portals enable you to search all of the properties available in your target area, regardless of which company is marketing it. These websites are free for buyers to use, and you can search as much as you like. (Instead of scrolling social media, Cory enjoys flicking through the Rightmove app after dinner for a bit of light research!)

Within these portals you are able to specify and save a search area along with various other criteria, meaning that you will be emailed the minute a new listing is added that fits your parameters. Once you find a property you're interested in, you can send an email request to find out more, or call the estate agent directly. These portals are used by the most reputable agencies.

> **TIP: If an agent doesn't use any portals, it is best to steer away from them. It is also best to refrain from free listing sites such for property purchasing: it's risky, unprofessional and carries no protection from dodgy vendors.**

When starting your search, we would suggest enquiring about five to 10 places initially via the portals. Make sure you base your shortlist on your property star (Chapter 4), taking into account what is really important to you.

Once you have made an enquiry via the portal, you will be put in touch with the agents marketing that particular property. Consider taking a half-day or full day to view the property during a weekday, as agents are less busy then and can give you more attention.

During the short listing process it's important to ask the right questions in order to get all of the relevant information and make your viewings as efficient as possible. Questions you may want to include are as follows.

Viewing checklist

1. How long has it been on the market?
The longer a house has been on the market, the more people that have viewed it and not bought. Consider that there may be a reason for this – it's important to find out what that reason is.

2. Have there been any offers yet?

If there have been rejected offers, it's important to find out the price. This way you can gauge the vendor's expectations against your own, which will help you when putting in your offer.

3. Is the vendor flexible on price?

An agent will not waste their time showing you a property if they don't believe you will buy it. If you're viewing a property that is over your budget, be honest with the agent and ask if the vendor will consider offers under the asking price.

4. Why are they selling?

Knowing the reason behind a sale helps you understand the vendor's psyche. The estate agent may not always be 100% honest with you, but it's always worth asking this question. For example, a couple with a new baby versus a retiree downsizing will have very different attitudes towards selling, and it helps to know what you're dealing with.

5. What is the vendor's position?

This is extremely important. The ideal scenario is a vacant or tenanted property. This means that there is no **chain** to rely on which could hinder or halt the sale, as the vendors also might be looking for somewhere to buy themselves (see Chapter 6). A chain occurs when the vendor needs to sell their property in order to purchase another. Although there is not much you can do to avoid a chain (apart from not buying the property), this is definitely something to be aware of, and avoided where possible.

If you do find a property embroiled in a chain, try to use it to your advantage. If the vendors have found a property they love, they might be willing to take a lower offer in order to move forward with their own purchase.

6. How long is the lease?

Do not buy a property with a lease under 80 years. Once a property drops below this time frame, it can cost tens of thousands of pounds to renew, plus high legal costs. Low lease properties tend to be marketed very cheap for this reason, and it is not worth the hassle unless you seriously know what you are doing.

7. How many viewings has the property had so far?

This will help you to estimate the level of interest in the property. If there have been loads of viewings in a short period of time, you need to get in quick. Conversely, if there have been lots of viewings over a long of time but no sale, it may indicate an issue with the property. If there has been little interest, it may indicate that the property is overpriced.

8. How much are the council tax, service charge and ground rent?

These are costs you need to be aware of when making your decision, as they will contribute to your monthly expenses (see also Chapter 2).

9. Have any offers fallen through, and if so, why?

If there is something wrong with the property, this could be a good indicator.

10. Are there any restrictions on pets?

Some developments do not allow pets as part of the head lease, so if you have a pet or are planning to get one, you will need to know this information from the outset. It would be a shame to purchase a lovely new one-bedroom flat in the best location and with the highest numbers on your star chart, only to find out that poor Tabitha the Tabby will not be coming with you!

11. Are there any major works planned?

You want to know if there are any upcoming works which could leave you out of pocket, or living on top of a building site. This is particularly pertinent in new-build developments which are part of a wider regeneration scheme.

We have friends who purchased a flat with a lovely balcony off the reception area, only to find out six months later that a huge site outside their window would be excavated in order for the next block to be constructed. Moreover, when the construction is complete after two years, they will be looking directly into their neighbours' living room!

12. Which way is the property facing?

Because the Earth spins anticlockwise, the sun rises in the east and sets in the west. Also, because the UK lies at a high latitude from the Equator, the sun shines from the south. This effect is more dramatic in winter than summer. As a result, south-facing properties get a lot of light in the daytime, which is ideal. If your property faces a different direction, take the amount of sunlight that you will get at different times into account. If you're facing east, you will get morning sun. West equals evening sun, and north generally will not get any direct sunlight shining into the windows, and so most likely will be dark throughout the day for the majority of the year.

This is by no means an exhaustive list of questions, and you may not want to ask them all at once but it's a great springboard to start with.

TIP: Remember: there is no such thing a silly question. This is your home, and you're entitled to have as many queries as you need!

How to conduct your viewings

There is a real art to the viewing process, and it's important to keep an eye on your progress as you move forward. As an agent, Cory sees a lot of different types of buyers: often people end up doing viewing after viewing without finding the right property.

The most common styles of purchasers are listed below. Have a look and see if one of these might be you!

The Nitpicker

Has an extremely long list of criteria which are all 'extremely important'. They are over-critical of everything, and never make an offer, as no property ever seems good enough. Agents tire of the Nitpicker quickly, as nothing they present will ever be suitable. This person will search for years before finding somewhere – if ever!

The Eager Beaver

Is extremely excitable and loves the house-buying process. They seem to be a good buyer, as they're open to everything and will make an offer quickly, only to rescind it when reality sets in and they realise it doesn't quite suit them. The Eager Beaver is easy for agents and vendors alike to manipulate.

The Checklister

Is open to viewing everything, but has a long list of questions and loves ticking them off. Although this is a good strategy, the Checklister can see things as black or white, focusing on their long list rather than how they *feel* about a place. This means that they can miss out on properties that are actually good options for them, due to the fact it hasn't ticked X amount of boxes.

The Timewaster

This person views loads of properties with no intention to buy. They won't have gotten their mortgage sorted, and probably won't even have saved a deposit. The Timewaster will not be able to buy a property at this time, so should not be out on viewings!

The Ditherer

The Ditherer is constantly afraid of missing out, and has what psychologists call 'commitment issues'. They're always paranoid about making an offer, as they're worried that a better property could be just around the corner, and so fail to make any decision at all. Needless to say, they usually end up in a long, unproductive and wasted search.

The Confident Consumer

The Confident Consumer is clear about what they want from the outset, but understands that no property will be 100% perfect. They have an open mind, but stay focused on their goals, not allowing themselves to be swayed by the agent. They have a healthy mix of practical application (asking the right questions) and following their gut.

Often, this type of purchaser will be successful in their property search – and they're the type of buyer you should aim to be!

What to look for when going on viewings

Once you've got your initial viewings booked in, it's important to make the most of them. You always want to view a place at least twice before committing to buy – more if possible. Bear in mind that you are not aiming to make any offer based on a single viewing, simply narrowing down the shortlist and taking no-goers off the table.

The first viewing

The first viewing is an ideal platform to get a feel for the place and have a springboard for comparison. Things to look for on a first viewing include the following.

The neighbourhood

Have a look around the area and the road. Notice how you *feel* when you arrive (calm, scared, stressed) – our intuition usually tells us more about the area then even the best presented set of property details.

The exterior

Look around the street, taking in any communal areas. Are they well maintained? Is the grass mowed? Are the bins empty or overflowing?

The interior

Examine the layout. Can you picture your belongings fitting in nicely? Is there enough space for you? (Don't be afraid to have a look inside cupboards or built-in wardrobes). Consider the overall flow: does the arrangement make sense to you? Have a look out of the windows – what is the view like, is it pleasing?

Another thing to look out for are signs of damp, such as condensation or creeping mould in corners. It's also good to test the water pressure. There's nothing worse than moving in somewhere and finding out you can't enjoy your usual bath or shower!

Make a shortlist

Once you've completed your preliminary list of properties, there are likely to be two or three places that really stick out for you: these are the ones to focus on. Put the others on the backburner for now, otherwise you will simply end up feeling overwhelmed.

At this point you can organise second viewings, and go through all aspects of the property with a fine-toothed comb. It's great to bring along a friend or family member at this point for a second eye.

The second viewing

Things to consider during the second viewing include:

* The floor plan – how will you layout your furniture? Will your sofa, bed and table fit nicely?
* The mortgage – how much will the monthly repayments be?
* The local area – how will your commute to work, social activities and/or your friends/family be?
* Area statistics – if you have children (or are planning to), this is the time to check out schools and nurseries in the area.
* The property at night – visit the property at different times of day (with or without the agent). Does it feel safe in the evening? Would you feel comfortable parking your car and/or walking home alone in the evenings?

Conclusion

The most important thing to remember during the whole process is to *keep the end goal in mind*. Focus on what you are looking for, and you can't go wrong. As we mentioned previously, after your first set of viewings, there should be two or three that pique your interest. After the second round has taken place, a clear winner should start to emerge. If not, no problem – cut your losses and take it back to square one.

If you've found the one, it's time to make your offer – we'll be talking about that in the next chapter.

Notes

Chapter 6

●　　●　　●

Making an Offer and Progressing the Sale

Exciting times! If you're at this stage of the book, there is a good chance you've found a property that you want to proceed with – which means it's time to make an offer.

In this chapter we'll be explaining exactly how to navigate the offer process, and discussing some of the key points to factor into it.

Talk to your agent

When you've decided on a price you would like to offer for a property, the first thing to do is to speak with your agent and discuss potential bids. Your agent will have built up a relationship with the vendor, and understands their motivation for selling – which means they're best placed to put your offer forward, and will have an idea of what the vendor will accept.

Gauging the right offer

You can gauge your chosen figure based on how long the property has been on the market, how keen the vendors are to sell, and previous offers that have been rejected. Ideally, you want to get the agent to suggest a price to you before you declare what you are willing to spend. You may be keen and able to go to the asking price, but don't let this slip straightaway: it's always good to start with a slightly lower offer then you're prepared to go to – you never know, they might just accept it!

Cory has seen a multitude of negotiation styles in his job, and sometimes he notices that the buyer will go into 'negotiation mode', becoming overly aggressive in order to seal the deal. Make sure this isn't you!

Take care to communicate courteously with the agent throughout the process. It's important to bear in mind that the agents want a sale (nearly) as much as you want to buy a house, so they will do the best they can to progress things.

Keep them sweet, build a good bond, and stay on their good side. There's often a chance that agents will be dealing with multiple offers, so they will be more likely to work closely with the applicants with whom they've got a good relationship – it's just human nature.

How to deal with counter-offers

If your offer is not accepted, then usually your agent will come back with a counter-offer from the vendor. If they don't give a figure away at this point, ask for one. The counter-offer will be less than the asking price, and you can decide at this point whether to proceed or try and haggle the price down further.

Some buyers try to squeeze every penny out of the sale to the death. This isn't a successful method, as what may save you a small amount a month on your mortgage may actually lose you a property due to needless back and forth, resulting in the vendor drawing a line and rejecting you altogether.

TIP: Decide on a price you are happy to pay, and work towards that with only two to three back-and-forth discussions maximum.

Sealing the deal

Once negotiations have ceased and a price has been agreed, then the deal is done! You will want to ask the agent to stop marketing the property, and to cease all viewings as part of the offer. Some vendors do continue viewings while a sale is agreed, in the hope of receiving a better offer. Although this is somewhat unethical, it's not actually illegal – so it's best to agree with the agent that this will not be the case.

Sorting the paperwork

Memorandum of sale

Once you've agreed a price with the vendor, the agent will send you a **memorandum of sale** which confirms that your offer has been accepted. It is at this stage that they will expect you to give them your solicitor's details, who will look after the legal side of the transaction.

TIP: If you can't find a solicitor, the estate agent may recommend a law firm with which they have a connection. This can be helpful, as the agent will have a good relationship with them already. This should help the process run as smoothly as possible to completion.

If you use a recommended firm, be sure to confirm their fees in advance, and compare them with a few other solicitors to ensure they are not charging over the odds. As soon as your solicitor starts work on the sale you will start to incur costs, so knowing what these are before instructing them is very important.

Along with details of your solicitor, the agent will ask for evidence of your mortgage agreement in principle, your mortgage broker's details, and sometimes proof of deposit. This is 100% legit and the agents' way of confirming that you are a bona fide buyer.

It's important to provide these details without delay, to show that you are a committed buyer. Any delay in providing documents or communication can cause nervousness on the agent or vendor's part, which can hinder relations and even risk their pulling out of the sale.

Going legal

Once you've started the process, your solicitor will begin work transferring the property from the vendor to yourself.

TIP: Remember: this is *not* the job of the agent, who is nothing more than an intermediary between both sides. The agent gets paid on completion of the sale, and will do their best to push things forward.

A solicitor gets paid irrespective of whether you complete the sale or not, and so they do not have the same level of motivation to progress things quickly. As a result, they may drag their heels, and it might appear as if there is no urgency on their part. It's important to speak with your solicitor often – every couple of days. This may seem awkward, but it's your property, and you have to stay on top of things.

Also, keep in contact with your agent, who should chase both sides if paperwork is left outstanding, or if there has been no contact from either parties for a while.

Once you've agreed the deal and get things moving, the process should take around six to 12 weeks from offer to collecting the keys. However, this may vary if you're buying a new build, or a development that is yet to be built. If you're lucky enough to be in a chain-free transaction, then you could be ready to move in within six to eight weeks.

Signing documents

Your solicitor will be responsible for making sure that you are informed about all the legalities of your purchase. This means that they (and the mortgage adviser) will send you a number of documents that you need to sign along the way. The quicker you complete and return documents, the better. Most delays in progressing a sale simply come from the buyer or seller being untimely with getting paperwork back to their respective solicitor.

> **TIP: Make sure you read all of the documents thoroughly, as these form the legal basis for ownership of your property. If there is anything you don't understand, talk to your solicitor or mortgage broker and ask them to explain it.**

There is nothing you should be unclear about when it comes to your own property.

Your mortgage documents

One of the most important documents you will receive from your mortgage broker is the **Key Facts Illustration (KFI).** This is a complete breakdown of the deal of your mortgage. Details found on the KFI will include the interest rate, duration and fees payable.

When we bought our first property we were unsure how to interpret this information, and ended up on a higher interest fixed rate mortgage when we had agreed a variable rate with our broker. As a result we ended up paying an extra £50 a month for absolutely no reason.

Take care to scour through the KFI with a fine-toothed comb to avoid silly mistakes like the one we made!

Once you've signed and returned each document, it's worth calling your estate agent to let them know and to ensure they're able to see if the vendor has done the same. They will appreciate the communication, and it will give them impetus to ensure the vendor is not falling behind.

Completing the sale

Towards the end of the process, your solicitor will ask you if you want to confirm a **completion date** and to **exchange contracts.** Once you've exchanged contracts you are legally bound to purchase the property, so there is no going back at this point. The completion date will be the day you pick up the keys from your agent, and the day your mortgage payments will start.

Other things to consider

Getting the most out of your survey

Once your offer is accepted, your mortgage company will need for you to have a survey done (see Chapter 2). Although it's an annoying expenditure, the survey is useful as it will give you a wealth of information about your chosen property.

The first flat we purchased was a 1990s purpose-built block that needed only minor cosmetic work before becoming liveable. We were on a tight budget and felt that as the property was relatively new, there wouldn't be many problems – so we decided to go with the cheapest option, i.e. the standard lender's valuation.

We were lucky that nothing untoward arose once we moved in, but in general we would always recommend doing a homebuyer's report at the bare minimum, so you know exactly what you are buying.

If there is anything you are worried about regarding the property you can ask the surveyor to look out for it specifically. Once you've received your report you can use any issues brought up to negotiate the price, or to ask the vendor to carry out remedial works before you agree to progress the sale.

Our second property was a maisonette with a loft. We were concerned about the possibility of vermin, so we asked our surveyor to carry out a homebuyer's survey and to specifically look for evidence of rodents.

Our report showed mouse droppings present, so we requested that the vendor carry out a full pest control service on the maisonette before we progressed. Luckily he agreed, and we felt much more comfortable about taking things forward and subsequently moving in.

Having said that, you need to be very careful about requests and renegotiation on the price at this point. Only fight the battles that are worth fighting at this stage, as any renegotiation can suggest to the vendor that you are untrustworthy – they may reject your offer completely. If something aesthetic comes up, it may be worth simply making plans to rectify them yourself.

Chains

As we mentioned in Chapter 5, chains can be tricky to navigate and can cause delays.

> **Example**
>
> If the property that the vendor is acquiring falls through, the chances are your own purchase will be affected. This gets more tricky if there are multiple people involved: say, if the vendor's new home is owned by sellers who also need to move, and so on.

As mentioned previously, the ideal scenario is to purchase from a chain-free vendor (perhaps someone moving abroad or a landlord); however, often this is not the case. As chains can be unavoidable, we wouldn't want you to miss out on your chosen property simply to avoid them, so don't worry about them too much. A chain sale should still go through relatively smoothly, but there is a higher risk of it taking a bit longer. It's important to stay in constant communication with your agent, so you can keep up-to-date about the various links of the chain as the sale progresses.

Fall-throughs

The process of buying and selling a property is not legally binding in England and Wales until the sales contract is signed and exchanged by both parties. Unfortunately, this means that at any point during the process, neither party is obligated to complete the sale. This makes the process very nerve-wracking for both sides, particularly as they will start to rack up costs for surveys, solicitor's fees and local authority searches.

There are various reasons why a sale may fall thorough. One of the most common is due to a change in the individual circumstances of either the buyer or vendor. You're buying from human beings and as we all know, human behaviour can be unpredictable.

Reasons that a fall-through may occur include the following.

The vendor may:

* decide to give a separated relationship another go, and choose not to sell
* regret the price they've agreed on, and try to secure a higher offer
* decide to rent the property out instead.

The buyer may:

* not be able to secure their mortgage
* see something else they prefer
* find that the survey brings up a number of issues that they are unwilling to rectify.

These are just a few examples, and sadly a fall-through can happen at any point. However, there are a few hard-and-fast things you can do to try and prevent a fall-through occurring with your purchase.

1. **Communicate** – As mentioned previously, talk to your agent, mortgage adviser and solicitor often: every few days is ideal. This ensures that all parties know where they stand, and limits any miscommunication and unnecessary delays.

2. **Be prepared** – Make sure you've assessed the vendor's situation before you agree to the sale. This gives you the ability to pre-empt any issues that may arise, and address them before they become larger issues.

3. **Be responsive** – Send all paperwork back within one to two days: this means that there are no hold-ups. Hold-ups suggest uncertainty, and might result in the vendor developing cold feet.

4. **Be transparent** – Be honest and clear with your mortgage broker from the outset. There is little point hiding a massive credit card bill in the hope that no one will find out. Your mortgage company will look into everything, so it's better to disclose all financial information at the beginning to avoid your mortgage offer being rescinded.

5. **Keep calm** – This is easier said than done, but it's extremely important to avoid pinning all your hopes on the sale and allowing it to rule your life. Make sure to keep living life, having fun and staying social during the process. This is very easy to forget!

What to do if your vendor pulls out

Should the vendor decide not to progress, see if you can uncover the reasons behind it. If there is anything you can do to change their mind, make sure to try your darndest. However, if the vendor is using a fall-through as blackmail to get you to raise your price, resist this highly unethical behaviour.

In recent years a trend of 'gazumping' has arisen. This is when a buyer accepts a purchase price, but before the sale is completed the seller accepts a better offer. This can result in the buyer losing money on surveys and solicitors' costs. Although frowned upon, this behaviour is not illegal in England and Wales.

> **TIP: Don't allow yourself to be bullied into paying more if you do not believe it is right. Trust your gut: as much as you love a property, there will always be another one out there that is right for you.**

If you do experience a fall-though, it's important not to let any negativity kill your enthusiasm for your entire search. For every sale that falls through, many more progress glitch-free, so don't give up! If you are committed to buying a home, simply chalk it up to experience and, when you feel ready, get back out there and start looking.

During this interim period, it is important to avoid the tendency to blow your deposit on a fancy holiday or car to cheer yourself up. This will only make you feel worse in the long run and lead you away from your final goal. This can seem easier said than done, but trust us, it will all be worth it in the end!

What to do if you need to pull out

If for any reason you decide not to progress with the purchase, let your solicitor know immediately. This means that they will stop working on the file, avoiding more costs.

Once you have let your solicitor know, you will need to speak with your mortgage broker and estate agent. The agent will not be happy, and more often than not will try and convince you to change your mind. However, as long as you have not exchanged contracts, you are legally able to withdraw: if your decision has been made, be completely clear with your agent about the reasons, and state that it is your final decision.

Always remain polite and cordial – after all, you may be back out looking with this agent in the near future. Although it's uncomfortable to pull out of a property sale, it would be even worse to buy somewhere you are not 100% about – so once you've made your decision, take it as a life lesson and move on.

Conclusion

As you can see, there is a lot to consider when making an offer. If you play your cards right, the odds will be in your favour – hopefully securing you a good deal. Remember: keep your solicitor close, and your estate agent closer. Communication is key, and maintaining open channels will ensure that the process runs as smoothly as possible.

Notes

Chapter 7

●　　●　　●

Moving In and Moving Forward

Excellent! You've got your keys and started paying your mortgage. Now what?

When we bought our first property, we remember stepping into the house on the day after completion and feeling completely overwhelmed – we didn't know where to start! Luckily, we weren't in a rush to move in, and so were able to do our research and ask family members for help and advice – but that isn't always an option for many people.

This chapter will cover the main things to think about when moving in, as well as ideas to consider for your future property journey.

Moving in

Bills, bills, bills...
Bills can be a forgotten part of the independent living process, but they're super-important and need to be sorted as an immediate priority.

Ensure that you do the following:

* Set up accounts with utility suppliers: gas, electricity and water
* Register your new address with TV Licensing (if you already have a TV licence; if you don't, you'll need to buy a new one)
* Register with your local council for council tax
* Set up your phone, TV (if desired) and broadband supply.

TIP: You can set up utilities by comparing the best options online. If this seems like too much of a hassle, an easy way to do this is by asking your solicitor for a list of current suppliers to the property, calling each provider and setting up an account starting from the date of completion.

Even if you are not planning to move in straight away, as soon as you complete the purchase, the bills become your responsibility from that day onwards.

Gas and electricity providers may ask you for meter readings, so make sure that you know where your meters are within the property.

We couldn't find our utility meter for ages, and had to contact the vendors once we moved in to find out where it was. Luckily, they were able to help, but they could just have easily ignored us once the sale was completed!

Your mortgage and service charge should have been set up already via standing order or direct debit as part of completion of the sale. However, it is worth checking with your solicitor that your standing order has been set up for the service charge (if your property has one), and checking with your bank to confirm.

Where your property has a management company, it's also a good idea to call them to introduce yourself, and to let them know that you've moved in.

Furniture

Of course, how much furniture you start off with will be up to you! Items that you will definitely need include a sofa, bed and wardrobe.

When we moved into our first flat, we agreed a deal with the vendors to buy their sofa, mirror and dining room table. It was a lot easier then scouring the shops, and the items already matched the flat in terms of size and decor.

We were also able to pick up some good items secondhand from charity shops, such as the British Heart Foundation.

If you're buying brand new furnishings, please bear in mind that most furniture chains will have lengthy delivery times, as products can be made to order. This means that sometimes you might be waiting for up to three months for your sofa, bed or wardrobe to arrive. This can be really frustrating if your completion date is only two weeks away, so make sure to plan in advance – otherwise you could end up sleeping on a blow-up mattress and eating dinner off cardboard boxes!

Refurbishment

Once you're in your own property, you are free to refurbish it as you see fit (for the most part).

If you have purchased a flat (as opposed to a house), it is important to remember that you are a leaseholder only. This means that you have a legal 'tenancy' and a freeholder to answer to – so make sure you check the details of your lease to find out exactly what you can and can't do within your new home.

Currently we live in a property with a loft. However, as leaseholders we are only allowed access to the *space within* the loft; we don't own the physical structure of the roof itself. This means that we are not allowed to convert the loft and extend the property, as we do not have any legal title to do this.

Had we not checked this and simply started work, the freeholder could have forced us through the courts to put the structure back to its original state – and we would have had to pay for that. We would have wasted a whole heap of money and energy, and for no reason.

Most decorative changes such as painting, hanging pictures and adding shelves will not require permission. However, larger projects such as removing walls, bathrooms or kitchens may need permission depending on the development. Again, just check your lease.

If you own a house and are the freeholder, as mentioned, you will be able to do most things without authorisation. However, loft conversions and extensions usually require planning permission from your local authority, so make sure to apply for permission before starting any work.

If you do organise any large-scale projects, coordinate them with any furniture deliveries to ensure that brand new furniture doesn't get covered in dust or paint – and if financially viable, organise a professional 'end of tenancy' clean before you move in.

The End of Tenancy Clean

This is the type of cleaning service that tenants use before they move out of a rental home: most professional cleaning companies provide them.

The service includes a team of up to five people blitzing the property thoroughly to ensure that all nooks and crannies are clean and fresh. They dismantle the oven, clean it with special chemicals, and put it back together again (the same with the extractor fan, if there is one, all kitchen appliances and the shower). They also steam clean carpets and upholstery as part of the cost. Moreover, as part of the service, should you not be satisfied with the overall standard of cleanliness or there are any particular areas of concern, they will send the team back for free to address this for you.

This means that when you are ready to move in, the property is absolutely spotless.

We found that spending £150 on a professional cleaning service before we moved in was a massive weight off our shoulders, as we knew we would be moving into a fresh and clean home. It saved us many hours of hard work, and took real stress off our backs at a really hectic time. If your budget allows, we would 100% recommend having a professional clean done.

Moving forward

Keep an eye on the lease

It's important to keep an eye on your lease as the years go by. If you are approaching 80 years or fewer, we would strongly suggest contacting your solicitor to find out how you can extend the lease. The cost can vary from £5,000 or £6,000 up to tens of thousands, but the longer you have left on your lease, the cheaper it is to renew.

If you're unable to pay for this cost upfront, you can ask your mortgage provider to add it to the cost of your mortgage. This does mean that your monthly payments will increase, but by extending the lease you will have increased the value – and your equity will still be secure.

Adding value to the property

While you're living in your property, you will have the opportunity to add value as time goes by. This means that not only will you gain equity though appreciation, you can increase its worth also by adding your own personal touches. Here are some simple ways to add value to your home.

Renovation

When considering changes to your property, you need to think about how you can make future buyers pay top dollar. A good place to start is in the kitchen and bathroom: two rooms which, if left to fall into disrepair, change the feel of a property completely.

We've all seen houses with 1970s-style salmon or avocado bathroom suites that even our Nan would be ashamed of! This is a big no-go for many people, so if you have money for refurbishment, fitting a new kitchen and bathroom is first on the agenda.

> **TIP: Where possible, don't scrimp on quality. Generally speaking, the higher quality the material used, the more it will add to your overall property value.**

Funds permitting, luxury materials could include real stone worktops, real wood floors, etc. Of course, buying extravagantly is not always an option – so if you do choose cheaper options, make sure they are fitted well and that the work is completed to a high standard.

Maintenance and DIY

While you live in your property, keep up with any general maintenance and DIY. For example, if your door handle breaks, spend a few quid and get it fixed instead of ignoring it and getting used to opening the door with a clothes hanger (we've all been there!). The more that little imperfections build up, the worse your home will look – and it will cost a lot to do it all at once, when it is time to sell.

Also, have a think about what you didn't like when viewing your home. If there is something that is an eyesore but can be changed, change it. If you didn't like it, the chances are others won't either, and it will be a barrier to the potential sales price. Examples could include an ugly front door, poor paintjob or a poorly fitted built-in wardrobe.

Decor

When it's time to sell, it's important that your decor is up to a decent standard. For example, make sure that carpets are not damaged, stained or overly worn. No one likes a grotty carpet, and a fresh carpet can really brighten a place up. New carpets are relatively cheap and can be easily fitted.

TIP: When decorating, be careful if you have a quirky style. While you might love having, say, a slide from one floor to another instead of stairs, that might not be for everyone!

Eccentric decor reduces your market of potential buyers, leading to a lower price, as the property will not be in demand.

Financial planning

When you become a homeowner, most likely your property will become your main asset. The value of this asset can go up or down, but as previously mentioned, the tendency is for property to double every eight years on average. In essence, you can become inherently richer without working late or pushing for that promotion. It simply happens via living your life and paying your mortgage on time.

Great, isn't it! A lot of people ask us how the money that is stored within their property can help if they cannot see or spend it. There are three main ways to release the value stored within your property:

1. Selling
2. Remortgaging and staying in the same property
3. Remortgaging and purchasing another property.

1. Selling

We hope you will have many happy years in your new home, but there may be a time when you are ready to move on. When you decide to sell, you will liquidate all of the accumulated equity into some well-deserved cash! You can then put this down as a deposit for another property (if you so choose).

This is the most common way to move up the property ladder, and allows you to buy higher-priced property without having to save up an enormous deposit. Just make sure to factor in any fees associated with the transaction, such as sales fees, solicitor's fees and general moving costs.

2. Remortgaging and staying in the same property

When your fixed-term mortgage offer comes to an end, you will be able to contact your mortgage adviser to look for a new deal. In the last three months of your current deal, get a few agents to value your property and ask them for *realistic* price (when remortgaging it's best to work with conservative figures). By this time it will have been two, three or five years since you initially bought, and the property value should have gone up.

> **Example**
>
> If you purchased a £200,000 property with a 10% deposit which has now increased to £220,000, then you will have made an extra £20,000.
>
> This means you will have doubled your return in two years (your initial investment being £20,000).

If, after this fixed period ends, you would like to continue living in the same property, often you can get a better deal from mortgage lenders as they will be happy to lend you the same amount of money but at a *lower* interest rate.

Lenders will see you as a safer bet, as you technically have a higher deposit to put down. The reason for this is that you've paid off some of your mortgage and your property price has gradually increased, creating a higher equity buffer. As a result your monthly payments should go down, which will be a nice little sweetener for you.

If you have any savings of your own to top up your deposit further at the remortgage stage, your payments will go down even more, making day-to-day life just that little bit easier.

TIP: Bear in mind that any savings that you put into your property are not 'spent' but stored – and in the future they'll

be giving you a lot more money in your pocket than staying static in a savings account.

3. Remortgaging and purchasing another property

Another option is remortgaging to release capital with the goal to reinvest. This has become a lot harder in recent years due to changes in tax law, and there are more changes planned.

This option works by pulling out any equity in your property which has been raised over the duration of your mortgage, to put a deposit down on another property. This sounds great in theory, but it's important to remember that property prices may have continued to rise around the country, and any cash you are able to release may not stretch very far.

If this is something you are considering, it's important to consult your mortgage adviser, to assess how much cash you could release from your property. There are two options you can use with this strategy: let to buy, and buy to let.

Option 1: Buy to let

This option is best when you are happy where you are living and don't want to move, but still want to reinvest the accumulated equity in the form of a new property.

With a buy to let you release equity from your current home to purchase another. In order for this to work you need to keep a certain amount of equity in your residential property. A residential mortgage may enable you to keep around 15%, depending on your situation and the market. Your mortgage adviser can guide you on this, and will find you a new mortgage deal on your current home as well as a buy-to-let mortgage for your new property purchase.

Provided that this all goes to plan, you will be able in effect to purchase a buy-to-let property that will start you off with a small portfolio, growing your net wealth through the models of equity and leverage. However, finding a residential lender willing to remortgage your current property at an 85% loan to value (LTV) with a 15% **equity stake** will be no mean feat! This is likely to increase your monthly repayments, and as the mortgage will be based on your salary, you may not be able to release a high amount of cash.

> **TIP: In April 2016, the Government imposed a 3% stamp duty levy on all buy-to-let investments – meaning that property developers now pay the standard stamp duty *plus* a further 3%.**

Remember, if you go down either of these routes, you will be starting the entire buying process again. This means that all the associated costs that come with buying a property will apply (solicitors' fees, stamp duty, moving costs, etc.). You also need to consider any renovations needed to turn a standard property into a rental one and all the other costs included with becoming a landlord, such as landlord insurance, management fees, professional cleaning and repairs.

It's crucial to have your finances in order, and to understand the law around lettings and self-assessment, as you will be solely responsible for everything to do with your rental investment. Owning a rental property is not for everyone. It is a huge responsibility, and these options take a lot of careful consideration and calculation.

Option 2: Let to buy

This is the exact opposite to the previous example. Often, this option is used when people have outgrown their current home and are ready to move on to another. The strategy here is to release equity from your property to use as a deposit for another place to live in, while renting out your current home.

Although you may have built up a large amount of equity in as little as five to 10 years, property prices will have risen simultaneously, so careful financial planning is required to execute this plan.

When you speak with your mortgage broker, they will give you an overview of the mortgage options available to you. Most lenders will want at least a 25% deposit (i.e. 25% of the total property value) to remain in your current property, meaning the deal that your broker will be searching for is a 75% LTV mortgage for your current property. In addition, you will need two types of mortgage for this option: a buy-to-let mortgage for the property you are renting out or leaving, and a residential mortgage for the property to which you are moving.

> **Example**
>
> Brokers are more concerned that the potential rental income will be at least 25% to 45% over the mortgage.
>
> So, if your monthly mortgage on the home you are renting out will be £1,000pcm, based on the deals that your mortgage broker can find, you will need to be able to secure a rental income of at least £1,250pcm.

It's also important to note that you will still need a decent salary to qualify for a residential mortgage for your new home, which *will* be reliant on your current income.

TIP: Many landlords following this route choose an interest-only mortgage for their rental property, as it will bring monthly payments down, providing a rental income. This means you will build equity due to property prices going up, as opposed to paying the mortgage down each month. Most professional landlords whom Cory has worked with structure their portfolios in this way.

Conclusion

What we have described in this chapter is a simplified model of how you can use property to invest in and build further wealth. There are many resources out there which provide a more comprehensive insight into property management and investment (you can check out our Resources section at the end of the book for more information). However, in this book we are only giving you an overview and a springboard for future research, hopefully providing some ideas to think about.

Notes

The End

So, here we are. We have reached the end, and what a journey it's been!

We hope you have learned a lot and gleaned some inspiration for the next steps on your property voyage. There is a wealth of knowledge out there for you to delve deeper into, and we hope this has proved to be a useful introduction.

Remember your final destination, and check in with your goal and action plans regularly. Write them down, stick them up somewhere easy to see, and share them with your loved ones to keep you on track.

Property is such an exciting business, and it's only set to get better. We're passionate about the benefits that home ownership can bring, and we're super-fanatical about supporting our peers to get there.

We wish you the best of luck with your property purchase, and cannot wait to find out how you get on. Make sure to let us know!

You can find us at:

Website: www.howtoformillennials.com

Instagram: How_To_Buy_A_Property

The ache of home lives in all of us, the safe place where we can go as we are and not be questioned.

Maya Angelou

Acknowledgements

L ildonia:

This book was a labour of love.

First and foremost I would like to thank my loved ones; my wonderful family and closest friends who support me with all of my ventures. This book is one of the most exciting things I have ever written and I would not have been able to do it without all of you.

A thank you to our editor Lisa Cordaro for her insight, professionalism and patience. You have made this process extremely smooth and stress free.

Every life coach needs a coach of their own and so I would also like to thank my coach Adam Awan for his support, inspiration and guidance throughout this process.

This book is self published and so I would like to thank Amazon, for allowing us independent writers to do our thing!

As always, I am so grateful to the Universe for guiding me on this amazing path.

Last but not least I would like to offer a multitude of gratitude to my wonderful husband Cory McNally for working with me on this project and introducing me to the joys of property. It has been a pleasure.

Glossary

Bank of England Base Rate Bank of England tariff set as the standard interest rate for mortgages across the UK. Always expressed as a percentage, and varies based on the wider economy at the time.

Capital payments The portion of a monthly mortgage payment that decreases the total amount owed.

Cash buyer An individual purchasing a property who is paying the total sum in cash.

Chain Occurs when either a buyer or vendor still needs to buy or sell their property for the sale to progress.

Commercial lender A bank or other financial institution offering mortgages to the public.

Commercial units Space designated for shops and/or restaurants.

Completion date The date on which the sale of a property is finalised. Also when the buyer receives the keys.

Council swap A process where two council tenants swap their properties with one another.

Equity

The difference between the value of a property and the mortgage.

Equity loan

A current UK government house buying scheme where a percentage of the property value is *loaned* to an individual who meets specific criteria. The same *percentage* must be paid back after a number of years.

Equity stake

The amount of equity stored within a property.

Exchange contracts

The point within the property purchasing process where the transaction becomes legally binding.

First refusal

The privilege of deciding whether to accept or reject a property before it is offered to others.

Flipping

Purchasing a property and selling it on quickly with the sole aim of profit. Often involves major or minor renovations to increase value.

Freeholder

A type of property ownership in the UK granting *unconditional* rights over a building and/or land that the building sits on. Often associated with houses.

Head lease	The contract between all legal owners of a housing development and the freeholder.
Interest	The fee that a mortgage lender charges for loan of funds. Often expressed as a percentage.
Interest rate	The cost that a mortgage lender charges to take out a mortgage, expressed as a percentage of the total value of the mortgage.
Key Facts Illustration	A document issued to an individual taking out a mortgage, listing core details about the product.
Kerb appeal	How attractive a property looks from the exterior.
Lease	The long-term contract that an 'owner' of a property (usually an apartment) has with the freeholder of that property.
Leaseholder	A type of property ownership in the UK granting *conditional* rights over a property based on the terms of a long-term lease (contract). Often associated with apartments.
Leverage	Using borrowed capital to increase the potential return on an investment. The higher the proportion of borrowing, the higher the leverage.

Loan to value (LTV)	The proportion of the value of a property covered by a mortgage, expressed as a percentage.
Memorandum of Sale	Document issued by an estate agent confirming the core details of a property transaction.
Mortgage repayment	The amount paid to the mortgage lender each month.
Mortgage term	The duration of a mortgage. Often offered as 25, 30 or 35 years on a new mortgage.
New build	A newly-constructed property. Also refers to a style of architecture associated with properties recently built.
Off-plan	A property not yet constructed, but with full architectural plans and projections.
Repossess	Ownership of a property is transferred to a mortgage lender when an individual defaults on their mortgage payments.
Repossession	A property legally owned by a mortgage lender, due to the original owner defaulting on their mortgage.
Remortgage	Securing a new lender to pay off an existing mortgage on a property, to move forward on a new financial arrangement.

Retail Price Index	A common measure of economic inflation.
Right to Buy	A scheme allowing council tenants to purchase their council-owned property.
Service charge	A payment attached to a property paid to a freeholder or managing agent for communal works and services.
Staircasing	Purchasing a greater percentages of a shared ownership property.
Subsidence	Gradual movement of land under a property, often creating serious structural issues.
The Matrix	The 'rat-race' of modern day society (colloquial term).

Resources

Further reading

David Lawrenson, *Successful Property Letting: How to make money in buy-to-let*, Robinson, 2015.

Ian Samuels, *Property Tycoon: A simple seven-step guide to becoming a property millionaire*, Harriman House, 2014.

Online resources

Architects Registration Board (ARB)
www.arb.org.uk

Association of Residential Letting Agents – ARLA Propertymark
www.arla.co.uk

Bank of England
www.bankofengland.co.uk

CLC – The Specialist Property Law Regulator
www.conveyancer.org.uk

Financial Conduct Authority (FCA)
www.fca.org.uk

Fiverr
www.fiverr.com

Money Saving Expert
www.moneysavingexpert.com

Money Super Market

www.moneysupermarket.com

National Association of Estate Agents – NAEA Propertymark

www.naea.co.uk

Really Moving

www.reallymoving.com

Rightmove

www.rightmove.co.uk

Royal Institution of Chartered Surveyors (RICS)

www.rics.org/uk

Spare Room

www.spareroom.com

Spending Tracker app

https://play.google.com/store/apps/details?id=com.mhriley.spendingtracker&hl=en (android)

https://itunes.apple.com/gb/app/spending-tracker/id548615579?mt=8 (Apple)

Zoopla

www.zoopla.co.uk